THE HOME EDIT

Workbook

PROMPTS, EXERCISES,
and ACTIVITIES *to* HELP YOU
CONTAIN *the* CHAOS

CLEA SHEARER & JOANNA TEPLIN

CLARKSON POTTER / PUBLISHERS

NEW YORK

GET THE BESTSELLING BOOKS THAT HAVE TRANSFORMED THOUSANDS OF HOMES

 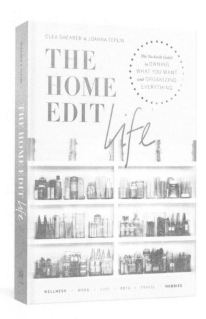

"If you ever see an incredibly organized pantry or enviably neat closet from your favorite celebrity on Instagram, it's probably the work of Clea Shearer and Joanna Teplin, co-founders of *The Home Edit*. These professional home organization experts—yes, that's a thing!—live for color-coded shelves, matching baskets, and labeled jars to help their A-list clients achieve organization nirvana."

—THE *TODAY* SHOW

THIS WORKBOOK BELONGS TO:

_____

Contents

Introduction

We're all for decluttering. But you don't have to live like a minimalist to feel organized. It's okay to own things—your things serve a very real purpose and deserve a space in your home. Maybe they help you keep your home clean or your kids alive. Or maybe some of your things are simply there because they make you happy, and that's a good enough reason to keep them. But here's the catch: You need a place to put all those things. They need to be easy to find, ideally at a glance. And you have to be able to maintain your system for storing them, or what's the point of it all?

In decluttering hundreds of homes, we've learned a ton of organizing tricks along the way. So let's team up! In this workbook, we've divided the typical home into categories so you can tackle your things-to-space ratio in a manageable way *before* the piles get so high you're left with no room to breathe. Each chapter helps you conquer one room or area, like the kitchen or your bedroom. And within each chapter smaller challenges break down that room or area into zones, like the fridge or the dresser. But here's the deal: You know your home best! So, first choose a chapter (it doesn't have to be chapter 1) and dive in. Jumping around from zone to zone within each chapter has our stamp of approval. It's just plain realistic. And if one room or zone doesn't apply to your home? Skip it.

Tip: We suggest beginning with the easiest challenge, The Junk-No-More Drawer (page 10). That's also where you'll find our how-to on Home Editing your space, tips you'll want to implement throughout the entire house.

Once you've chosen the chapter where you want to start, flip through the challenges and rank them in this very simple way: On a scale from one to ten, rate the space's mess at the top of the page. Then start with the challenge you gave the lowest number. Always tackle the smallest messes first. Gradually you'll work your way up until, check, that chapter's done and you can kick up your feet before you're ready for the next one. Each challenge and each chapter gets easier once you find your rhythm. You don't need to be as obsessive about organizing as we are. You just need to develop a system that works.

Along the way we'll check in to help you think about how you want each space to make you feel. You'll get to write lists—are we the only ones who do a happy dance every time we check something off one of our lists?—answer fun questions about yourself, and sketch some plans (IN PENCIL PLEASE! Unless you're an architect, in which case you'll probably nail it on the first try).

You've totally got this. And if you're feeling overwhelmed, you're in the right place, because conquering clutter and making homes pretty—it's kind of our thing. But trust us: When it comes to organizing, if we can do it, you can do it. It's easier than you think, and we're going to have a blast—you'll see.

—Clea and Joanna

How to Sketch Your Space

Many of these challenges ask you to sketch a specific space to scale using the gridded paper provided. Don't let this intimidate you! Using gridded paper as a way to determine furniture placement on floor plans is pretty common. But you can apply the same method to smaller spaces—like the interiors of drawers, cabinets, and closets—so you can maximize your storage containers and your things in the space.

To do so, measure your space with a tape measure and determine the best ratio of real-life space to gridded paper space. It's similar to what you might have seen on a map key back in the day: one foot of real space might equal one little square on the gridded paper. Then, keeping the ratio in mind, draw your space to scale on the gridded paper provided. Write down the ratio so you don't forget.

⊢⊣ = 1 ft.   ⊢——⊣ = 2 ft.   ⊢———⊣ = 3 ft.

CHAPTER 1

THE KITCHEN

A kitchen can be a stumbling block, but that's just because it's such a massively important part of your home. (No pressure, right?) Before you start breathing into a paper bag, remember: We're breaking it down into sections. But first, let's snack, er, reflect . . . Reflect, then snack!

What do you love most about your kitchen?

_____

_____

_____

_____

_____

What is your kitchen missing that could make it feel more functional?
More beautiful?

_____

_____

_____

_____

_____

How do you want to feel when you're in your kitchen?

_____

_____

_____

_____

_____

What does your kitchen need less of? What could it use more of?

_____

_____

_____

_____

_____

THE JUNK-NO-MORE DRAWER

RATE THIS MESS: ○ ○ ○ ○ ○

When anyone asks us where to start in the home while first beginning to organize, we always say *start with a drawer*. Not a closet, not a cabinet, but a simple drawer (and preferably a shallow one). Enter: the junk-no-more drawer. It's easy enough to tackle and stay motivated, but it can really make a difference in your state of mind. Look, your first attempt at tidying your house is hard enough, so start small. You'll thank yourself later.

So open that kitchen junk drawer and begin. As long as everything is contained, categorized, and makes sense in your daily routine, we'll call it a win.

THINGS YOU NEED TO GET RID OF

_____

_____

_____

_____

WAYS TO BEAUTIFY THIS SPACE

_____

_____

_____

_____

THINGS THIS SPACE COULD USE

_____

_____

_____

_____

How to Home Edit

1. Pull everything out of the drawer and lay it on the floor or counter.

2. Divide all of the things into categories, for example, writing utensils, batteries, paper pads, and charging cords. You can be as broad or as specific as you want with your categories—as long as they make sense to you.

3. Chuck whatever is old, grimy, broken, or not inspiring, like that free pen you got from your accountant that you never use because you hate the way it writes.

4. Brainstorm ways to store these items, researching containers you might need to buy or ones around the house that you might reuse (such as sturdy packaging that comes with a new gadget). Add them to your things-this-space-could-use list at left.

5. Proceed to the next page.

TRY IT! Using the gridded paper below, plan out your drawer space by drawing its dimensions (see page 7).

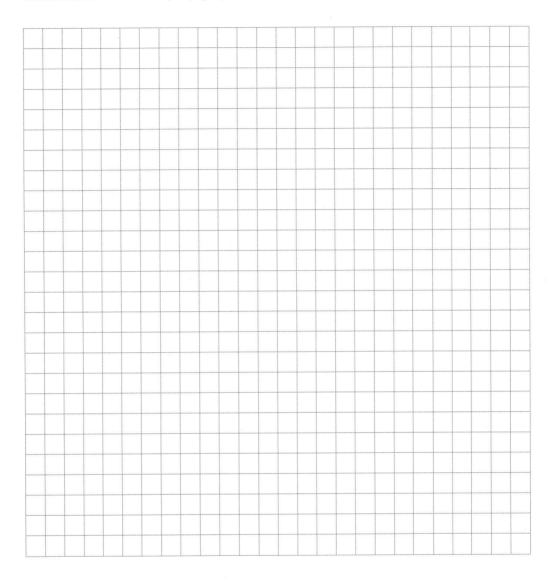

Collect your containers. Beautify your space. Organize your things. Take a deep breath.

You're done. How did it go? Capture your thoughts here:

_____

_____

_____

However you did, give
yourself a gold star.

THE FRIDGE & FREEZER

RATE THIS MESS: ○ ○ ○ ○ ○

Cleaning out your fridge might be the most transformative organizational project you do in your home. Don't be surprised if, after finishing this project, you begin to reap all kinds of health benefits. You might finally get the urge to cook dinner—just go with it.

This is a space that, when thoughtfully organized, really delivers. Once you get rid of those crusty mustard jars and expired jellies, you'll be ready to hit the grocery store to stock up on fresh fruits and veggies and live your healthiest life, whatever that means to you. Because you will know exactly what's in your fridge and when it will go bad, you'll also find yourself wasting less and saving money by not buying unnecessary items. Let's get started.

THINGS YOU NEED TO GET RID OF

_____

_____

_____

WAYS TO BEAUTIFY THIS SPACE

_____

_____

_____

THINGS THIS SPACE COULD USE

_____

_____

_____

RECIPES YOU HOPE TO BE INSPIRED TO TRY

_____

_____

_____

How to Approach the Fridge

1. Consider your cooking style. Think about how your household eats and be realistic. In addition to cleaning out expired foods, you'll also want to cull anything you probably won't eat or anything you want to prepare before it eventually expires.

2. Empty it out and give it a good scrub. Getting the inside of the fridge to sparkle is a chore since any spills tend to harden with the cold temps. Say no to harsh chemicals, but yes to hot, soapy water.

3. Consider containing everything that might leak, spill, or tip over. Use clear containers so you can easily spot what you're looking for.

4. Think about your categories based on the food and drink you typically stock and then label those categories on your containers and the fridge drawers.

5. Adjust the shelves, if possible, to fit your individual storage needs. Add the contents back to the fridge, using labeled containers as needed.

Using the gridded paper below, plan out your fridge and freezer spaces by drawing their dimensions (see page 7).

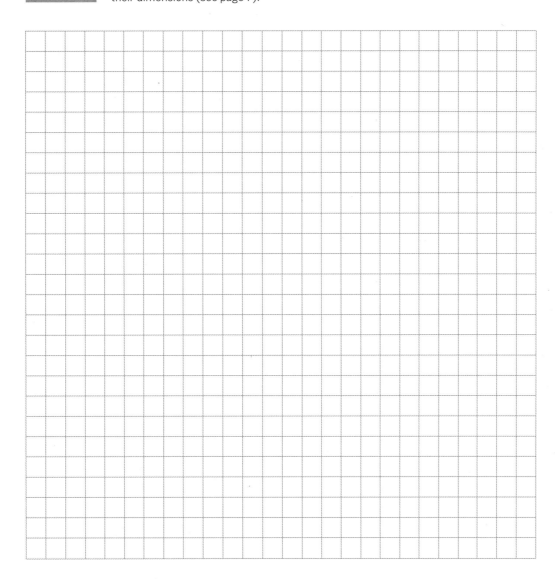

Collect your containers. Beautify your space. Organize your things. Take a deep breath.

You're done. How did it go? Capture your thoughts here:

_____

_____

_____

However you did, give
yourself a gold star.

THE UNDER-THE-SINK STORAGE

RATE THIS MESS: ○ ○ ○ ○ ○

Just about everyone has the cabinet equivalent of a junk drawer under their kitchen sink—a space that holds a mishmash of cleaning supplies, extra garbage bags, and maybe even the garbage can. Sometimes this space can be a blank canvas with little to no shelving and, to add insult to injury, there's an awkward pipe running through the whole space. So how do you deal? Measure, measure, measure. Then, research the types and sizes of organizers that can help you properly stow your things.

THINGS YOU NEED TO GET RID OF

_____

_____

_____

WAYS TO BEAUTIFY THIS SPACE

_____

_____

_____

THINGS THIS SPACE COULD USE

_____

_____

_____

THINGS YOU NEED EASIER ACCESS TO

_____

_____

_____

What's in Store

In order to optimize every inch under the sink, we use stackable bins to take advantage of the cabinet height (it helps if the bottom bin is actually a sliding drawer unit so that items remain accessible), and we line up supplies down the middle where the pipes are located. Here are some other ideas:

Wire racks or shelves that are adjustable to the various heights of the space and that can fit around the pipes

Over-the-door caddies to hold items you reach for again and again

Sliding shelves to alleviate all the squatting you do in this space (work smart, not hard)

Easy-to-clean containers because even cleaning containers need to be wiped down

Turntables (aka lazy Susans) for easy access in tight corners

Plastic shoeboxes or drawers to protect in case of a leak (you never know)

TRY IT! Using the gridded paper below, plan out your cabinet by drawing its dimensions (see page 7).

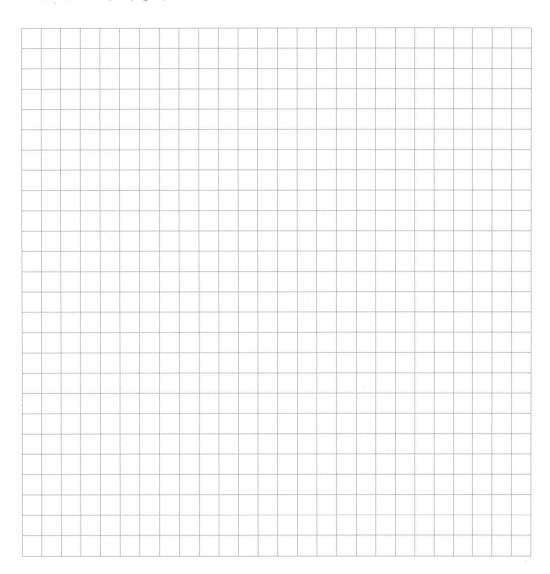

Collect your containers. Beautify your space. Organize your things. Take a deep breath.

You're done. How did it go? Capture your thoughts here:

_____

_____

_____

However you did, give yourself a gold star.

THE KITCHEN CABINET

RATE THIS MESS: ○ ○ ○ ○ ○

Pick a cabinet, any cabinet. Or tackle all of them in this challenge, if you're up to it. Depending on your cabinet design—whether you have glass-front doors or open shelving or if everything can hide behind a wooden cabinet front—you may have to be more strategic about beautifying the space. Even if everything is hidden behind the cabinet door, losing product packaging for canisters will make this space look infinitely better.

THINGS YOU NEED TO GET RID OF

_____

_____

_____

WAYS TO BEAUTIFY THIS SPACE

_____

_____

_____

THINGS THIS SPACE COULD USE

_____

_____

_____

WHO USES THIS CABINET THE MOST?

_____

_____

_____

_____

An Open and Shut Case

If you're in the market for new canisters, look for coordinating ones that can stack. Also, remember that some prefab cabinets have adjustable shelves. When you can change the height of a shelf to fit your needs, everybody wins. Here are more tips:

1. Don't let the shelves dictate your storage. Elevate your items with a tiered shelf, install pull-out shelves for lower cabinets, or bring in turntables (aka lazy Susans) to keep things from hiding in corners.

2. Consider how often you use something and prioritize what needs to stay within reach and what can go on the top or back of the shelves.

3. Rethink your categories in terms of zones for best functionality, such as creating a drink station with coffee, tea, mugs, and filters in a cabinet above your coffee maker or designating a weeknight makeshift pantry close to the stove containing quick-cooking components (like pasta, canned tomatoes, and olive oil).

4. Keep in mind your everyday needs, thinking about how you would like to store your goods. Do you really want to decant all your dry goods into labeled jars? If this is not a system you're willing to keep up, then consider something simpler.

TRY IT! Instead of drawing your cabinet layout, let's have a different kind of fun. In the space below, reflect on the following questions: What do you tend to discuss at the dinner table? Think back to the last great meal you had at home: What did you eat and who were you with? What were your three favorite meals when you were a kid? What are your top three refrigerator essentials? What are your top three pantry essentials? What is your dream kitchen appliance? What do you keep in your kitchen that might surprise your friends?

_____
_____
_____
_____
_____
_____
_____
_____
_____
_____
_____
_____
_____

Collect your containers. Beautify your space. Organize your things. Take a deep breath.

You're done. How did it go? Capture your thoughts here:

_____
_____
_____

However you did, give
yourself a gold star.

THE PANTRY

RATE THIS MESS: ○ ○ ○ ○ ○

There's no space we love to organize more than the pantry, but it tends to be the toughest spot in the house to organize. Whether your pantry is a cabinet or a whole closet, you'll probably be surprised to find a sea of pasta and cereal boxes. There will be expired foods and random cans of things that you thought you would use but that have not seen the light of day since they came home from the grocery store. Don't freak out. Just see this as an opportunity to restock with foods that you will actually eat or cook with.

THINGS YOU NEED TO GET RID OF

_____

_____

_____

WAYS TO BEAUTIFY THIS SPACE

_____

_____

_____

THINGS THIS SPACE COULD USE

_____

_____

_____

IDEAS FOR MAKING THE PANTRY MORE
USER-FRIENDLY

_____

_____

_____

How We Love to Organize a Pantry

With a pantry, you need to be disciplined with your steps. Unless you plan on throwing everything away and starting over, once you empty the pantry, you'll have to find a way to put it all back in. Here's a recap of The Home Edit process:

1. Take everything out and group it into piles (such as breakfast, dinner, and snacks) as you empty the space.

2. Go through each pile and toss anything that you don't like or use.

3. Organize the remaining piles into storage bins and containers, if using.

4. Arrange the groupings in your space in a way that's beautiful and makes sense for your household.

Using the gridded paper below, plan out the space by drawing its dimensions (see page 7).

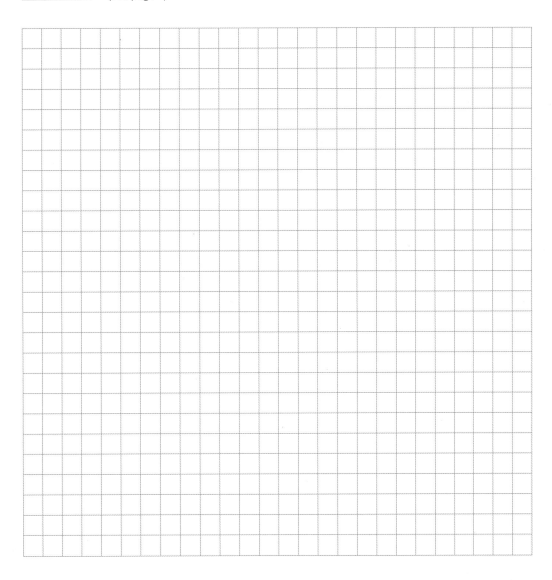

Collect your containers. Beautify your space. Organize your things. Take a deep breath.

You're done. How did it go? Capture your thoughts here:

_____

_____

_____

However you did, give
yourself a gold star.

THE NO-PANTRY SOLUTION

RATE THIS MESS: ○ ○ ○ ○ ○

We always tell you to start with a drawer, but sometimes you can *end* with a drawer, too. For this challenge, we want you to reenvision a drawer for a specific use. It can be the perfect spot to set up a snack station, beverage or breakfast supplies, or a spice solution. Think of what kind of drawer you need in your kitchen and get to it.

THINGS YOU NEED TO GET RID OF

_____

_____

_____

_____

WAYS TO BEAUTIFY THIS SPACE

_____

_____

_____

_____

THINGS THIS SPACE COULD USE

_____

_____

_____

_____

Surprising Drawer Possibilities

1. Transfer spices into uniform jars, then line them up in alphabetical order for quick ID.

2. Arrange grab-and-go protein bars and tea supplies (out of the boxes!) in separate compartments.

3. Line up snack bars, fruit pouches, and nuts in horizontal sections.

4. Position breakfast bars and instant oatmeal packets in vertical sections.

_____

_____

_____

_____

TRY IT! In the space below, list five ways you plan to live healthier once you've finished Home Editing your kitchen. (Hint: Your ideas don't all have to be food related!)

1. _____
_____

2. _____
_____

3. _____
_____

4. _____
_____

5. _____
_____

Collect your containers. Beautify your space. Organize your things. Take a deep breath.

You're done. How did it go? Capture your thoughts here:

_____
_____
_____

However you did, give
yourself a gold star.

THE KIDS' DISHES DRAWER

RATE THIS MESS: ○ ○ ○ ○ ○

We get asked a lot about what to do with kids' items in a kitchen. They always seem to be in unruly piles and make the inside of a cabinet look like a ROYGBIV bomb went off (that's Red, Orange, Yellow, Green, Blue, Indigo, Violet, for those who need a refresher). There are a few ways to make the dishes and sippies work, but one of our go-tos is a deep drawer. Bonus: Kids can help themselves! Let's reflect.

No kids? Use this space for your stemless wineglasses or any other grown-up glasses. Or how about a mixology drawer for oversize-ice-cube trays, shakers, muddlers, strainers, and corkscrews?

THINGS THE KIDS NEED MORE OF

_____

_____

_____

_____

THINGS THE KIDS NEED LESS OF

_____

_____

_____

_____

THINGS THIS SPACE COULD USE

_____

_____

_____

_____

Starting Lineup

Similar to a plating strategy for kids, nothing in this drawer should touch: Try to split up everything into different sections and find a way to contain all the disparate pieces.

1. Single-file dishes, snack bowls, and sippy cups in separate bins instead of stacking them.

2. Separate and compartmentalize bottle parts.

3. Organize utensils into cups.

_____

_____

_____

_____

TRY IT! Measure your drawer and determine how many compartments you can fit. Then, using the grid below, draw the way you want to organize it all (see page 7). Bonus points for having a little one create the sketch.

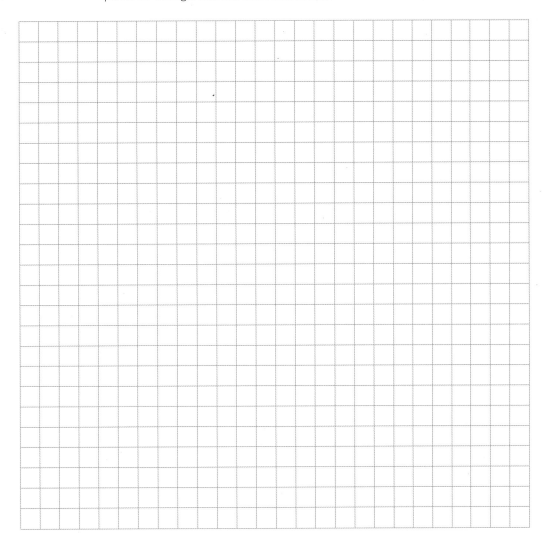

Collect your containers. Beautify your space. Organize your things. Take a deep breath.

You're done. How did it go? Capture your thoughts here:

_____

_____

_____

However you did, give
yourself a gold star.

THE CHINA CABINET

RATE THIS MESS: ○ ○ ○ ○ ○

For this challenge, pick the cabinet or case where you keep your nicest things. That might be a proper china cabinet, a glass-front cabinet for displaying decorative dishes or barware, or a cabinet shared with other kitchen essentials. Sometimes you need all the cabinet space you can get and you can't sacrifice prime shelving for dishes you never use. Two words for ya: coordinated canisters. These will elevate the essentials to look as nice as the entertaining pieces, so they can all sit together. But we need your glass to be half full. No, really! This is an instance where less is definitely more, so don't overdo it.

THINGS YOU NEED TO GET RID OF

_____

_____

_____

_____

WAYS TO BEAUTIFY THIS SPACE

_____

_____

_____

_____

FAVORITE DISPLAY-WORTHY DISHES

_____

_____

_____

Top Shelf to Bottom Shelf

You might be tempted to keep a lot of items on that top shelf, but if you do, it will appear cluttered. Similarly, while it's fine to keep food you use regularly on the bottom shelf, keep your canister layout clean and simple—just a few will do. Here's how we like to order shelf space from top to bottom:

> Rarely used entertaining platters and bowls
>
> Canisters of rice, pasta, and dry goods
>
> Canisters of baking sugars and flours (so they're closest to the stand mixer)

_____

_____

_____

What are a few things you hope will happen the next time you host a holiday? List them here. (Who will be there? What will you cook? Will you have a centerpiece? There are no rules!)

_____

_____

_____

_____

_____

_____

_____

_____

_____

_____

_____

_____

_____

_____

_____

Collect your containers. Beautify your space. Organize your things. Take a deep breath.

You're done. How did it go? Capture your thoughts here:

_____

_____

_____

However you did, give
yourself a gold star.

THE MORNING ROUTINE STATION

RATE THIS MESS: ○ ○ ○ ○ ○

Beverage setups are a few of our favorite things. Any space remotely within reason should have one. And, as part of an area devoted to your morning routine, what you create is a seamless way to start the day. If you're not a morning person, try to find the motivation to tidy this area and set it up every night before you go to bed, so the coffee can be waiting for you in the morning.

THINGS YOU NEED TO GET RID OF

_____
_____
_____

WAYS TO BEAUTIFY THIS SPACE

_____
_____
_____

EVERYONE'S FAVORITE BREAKFAST FOODS

_____
_____
_____

HOW YOU LIKE TO FEEL WHEN YOU START YOUR DAY

_____
_____

Good Day, Sunshine

Here are a few ideas for keeping things tidy in this space. You want to create a system that you'll maintain, so if these ideas aren't practical for your day-to-day, then figure out what is.

1. Transfer cereals, oatmeal, and pancake mix to glass canisters with scoops.

2. Display coffee beans in clear canisters (so you can see when you're running low and restock in time!).

3. Line up tea boxes in pull-out pantry drawers and organize them by ROYGBIV.

_____
_____

What's stressing you out right now? Brew some tea or pour some wine. Then get it all off your mind and down on this page.

_____

_____

_____

_____

_____

_____

_____

_____

_____

_____

_____

_____

_____

_____

_____

_____

_____

_____

_____

Collect your containers. Beautify your space. Organize your things. Take a deep breath.

You're done. How did it go? Capture your thoughts here:

_____

_____

_____

However you did, give
yourself a gold star.

CHAPTER 2

THE BEDROOM

Self-care, y'all. Tidying your bedroom is the equivalent of putting on your oxygen mask before helping everyone else. It'll make such a difference in your life (and in the lives of the people in your home). *Everyone* will thank us later, so be selfish and do it. Just remember to give yourself time to organize this space, as it tends to be scattered with emotional land mines and decision-making trip wires. You're going to find clothes that may no longer fit or that remind you of times long ago. You're going to wrestle with whether or not to keep the scarf your mother-in-law gave you. (Tip: Sell it online or donate it; SHE WILL NEVER KNOW.) Before we start, reflect on the following questions.

What's working for you in this room? What's not working?

_____
_____
_____
_____
_____

How could this room be more functional? More beautiful?

_____
_____
_____
_____
_____

How do you want to feel when you enter it?

_____
_____
_____
_____
_____

What does this space need less of? What could it use more of?

_____
_____
_____
_____
_____

A DRAWER

RATE THIS MESS: ○ ○ ○ ○ ○

We understand if you think you're ready to tackle the whole dresser, rather than just a single drawer. But we like to set the bar low for ourselves so we don't fail. We call this the Low-Bar Lifestyle. So we urge you to pick a single drawer in your bedroom—whether it contains socks and underwear or shirts—and save your energy for another day. We're just getting warmed up.

THINGS YOU NEED TO GET RID OF

_____

_____

_____

_____

_____

WAYS TO BEAUTIFY THIS SPACE

_____

_____

_____

_____

THINGS THIS SPACE COULD USE

_____

_____

_____

_____

Maximize Enclosed Spaces

1. Use in-drawer dividers to keep smaller items like socks organized. This also works for foldable accessories like bow ties and handkerchiefs.

2. Line sections for folded swimsuits and cover-ups to protect the delicate material.

3. Follow Marie Kondo's recommendation (if you haven't already read her book *The Life-Changing Magic of Tidying Up*, Google her "file folding" method) and turn stacks of clothing upright so you can see everything you have. You'll never have to turn your drawer inside out looking for shirts again!

_____

_____

_____

_____

_____

TRY IT! All dressed up with nowhere to go? No! Write down three places you plan to hit up in the next few months.

1. _____
_____
_____
_____

2. _____
_____
_____
_____

3. _____
_____
_____
_____

Collect your containers. Beautify your space. Organize your things. Take a deep breath.

You're done. How did it go? Capture your thoughts here:

_____
_____
_____

However you did, give
yourself a gold star.

THE DRESSER

RATE THIS MESS: ○ ○ ○ ○ ○

Now you're ready to tackle the rest of your folded clothes. Folks, this is where it gets real. Here's a hint to succeeding: Complete the editing step all at once, even if this means you need to finish the rest later. It's like trekking through the snowy woods. You're going to tell yourself that taking a break is necessary. Don't do it. You have to keep moving or you'll freeze to death. Stopping with the intention of restarting is a big reason people tend to lose interest and confidence when tackling an organizing project. Cull your clothes in one straight session; the beautifying piece can come later.

THINGS YOU NEED TO GET RID OF

_____

_____

_____

_____

WAYS TO BEAUTIFY THIS SPACE

_____

_____

_____

_____

_____

THINGS THIS SPACE COULD USE

_____

_____

_____

_____

_____

How to Purge

1. Have large black garbage bags already on hand. Designate some bags for trash, some for donations, and some for friends and family. Keeping your floor clear will help you stay motivated.

2. Make a plan for what you donate or give away. Knowing your exit strategy will strongly discourage you from keeping those bags around the house or in your car. You can always elect to phone a friend. Also, be realistic about what you intend to sell on eBay (are you really going to list it?).

3. Keep your project pile small. Things that need fixing (a watch with a broken link, pants that need hemming) should be attended to sooner rather than later so they can move back into their newly renovated home.

4. Consider storing or archiving. Can you store seasonal items on a higher shelf and make room for what you need now?

5. Take one more pass. Review what's left and make sure every single thing is worth your time and the energy it'll take to physically put it back in your space.

Once you've edited your dresser drawers and the dresser top, use the gridded paper below to plan out your dresser space (see page 7).

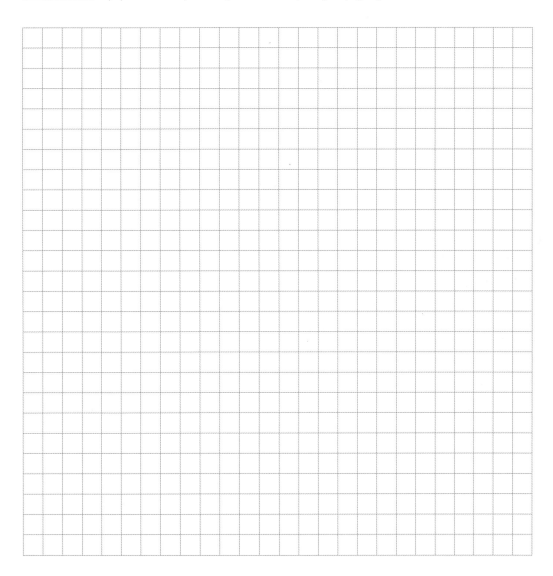

Collect your containers. Beautify your space. Organize your things. Take a deep breath.

You're done. How did it go? Capture your thoughts here:

_____

_____

_____

However you did, give
yourself a gold star.

THE BEDSIDE

RATE THIS MESS: ○ ○ ○ ○ ○

Everyone's bedside table is different, but if yours is not performing like your own personal butler, then you're missing out. Here's your chance to have a beautiful, functional space that will attend to your every need while you stay in bed. Let's make sure this space isn't cluttered with things you don't use or like. Keep it tip-top, so you can get a better night's sleep.

THINGS YOU NEED TO GET RID OF

_____

_____

_____

_____

_____

WAYS TO BEAUTIFY THIS SPACE

_____

_____

_____

_____

_____

THINGS THIS SPACE COULD USE

_____

_____

_____

_____

_____

My Bedside Checklist

TISSUE BOX COVER

WATER GLASS COASTER

VERTICAL BOOK STORAGE

READING-FRIENDLY LAMP
YOU LOVE

VASE

_____

_____

_____

_____

_____

What are your favorite books of all time? What was your favorite book during junior high? High school? College? Are there any you want to read again? What other books are on your to-read list? Are there any classics you've always meant to read?

_____   _____
_____   _____
_____   _____
_____   _____
_____   _____
_____   _____
_____   _____
_____   _____
_____   _____
_____   _____
_____   _____
_____   _____
_____   _____
_____   _____
_____   _____
_____   _____
_____   _____
_____   _____

Collect your containers. Beautify your space. Organize your things. Take a deep breath.

You're done. How did it go? Capture your thoughts here:

_____
_____
_____

However you did, give
yourself a gold star.

THE CLOSET

RATE THIS MESS: ○ ○ ○ ○ ○

When it comes to your whole house, but ESPECIALLY your closet, you should live by our 80/20 rule: Keep your home no more than 80 percent full, and reserve at least 20 percent for breathing room. Using all the available space is a bit like eating until you are overly full. It's as uncomfortable for your belt buckle as it is for your closet. You'll be happy for that extra breathing room when you spot a new dress you want to bring home.

THINGS YOU NEED TO GET RID OF

_____

_____

_____

_____

_____

WAYS TO BEAUTIFY THIS SPACE

_____

_____

_____

_____

_____

THINGS THIS SPACE COULD USE

_____

_____

_____

_____

How to Avoid Running Out of Space

1. Don't buy more hangers. You get what you get and you don't get upset.

2. Contain everything so you know when you've exceeded 80 percent of your designated space.

3. With every new purchase, ask yourself, "Where is this going to live?" If you don't have an answer, it doesn't go in your cart.

4. Set aside time once or twice a year to revisit and edit your spaces.

_____

_____

_____

_____

TRY IT! You'll find so many closet organizers to help you contain your things (think: over-the-door storage, hanging sweater organizers, and tiered shoe racks). But before you shop, use the gridded paper below to plan out the space by drawing your closet's dimensions (see page 7).

Collect your containers. Beautify your space. Organize your things. Take a deep breath.

You're done. How did it go? Capture your thoughts here:

_____

_____

_____

However you did, give
yourself a gold star.

CHAPTER 3

THE LIVING ROOM

There's something about the style of a living room that truly illustrates the personalities of the people who live there. If you were to take out all the furniture in your living room, would you put it back in the same exact way or would you opt for a different layout this time around? Here we'll look at that question and a couple of others.

What do you love about your living room?

_____

_____

_____

_____

_____

What is your living room missing that could make it more functional?
More beautiful?

_____

_____

_____

_____

_____

How do you want to feel when you're in your living room?

_____

_____

_____

_____

_____

What does this space need less of? What could it use more of?

_____

_____

_____

_____

_____

ALL ABOUT PHOTOS

RATE THIS MESS: ○ ○ ○ ○ ○

Unless you're a pro photographer, there's a good chance you haven't taken a pic on a device that isn't your phone in many, many years. But what about those old photos and photo albums collecting dust? There are many reasons why storing and organizing all of your photos digitally is a good idea. Not only is it a great way to share old images with others, but also THINK ABOUT IT: Are your children and grandchildren going to appreciate having to sort through and store numerous photo boxes filled to the brim? They will love you more for digitizing your collection now, so they don't have to deal with it later.

THINGS YOU NEED TO GET RID OF

_____

_____

_____

_____

_____

WAYS TO BEAUTIFY THIS SPACE

_____

_____

_____

_____

_____

THINGS THIS SPACE COULD USE

_____

_____

_____

_____

Let's Get Digital

1. Select a few photos to show off. Then promptly get them in frames and up on the wall or on your bookshelves before you forget.

2. Scan the rest, but consider using a local business or online service to do this for you. Life's too short to sit by a scanner all day.

3. Store all photo files on an external hard drive. That way, they won't slow down your computer and you can visit them anytime.

4. Use pretty photo storage boxes to preserve the backups in a closet or a shelf (never in the attic or basement where humidity can damage them).

5. Keep your photo folder system simple but descriptive. Naming folders generally—by year, location, or kid, for example—will help you keep up your momentum and steer clear of sentimentality, so you don't get stuck.

6. Edit to your heart's desire. Once everything is organized, you can select the ones you want to enhance, then show them off on social media. Note: Editing your hair in those '80s photos might be tough.

TRY IT! While you're going through old photos, award them with the following yearbook superlatives, then use the space below each to capture a memory.

★
THE BEST DRESSED

_____
_____
_____
_____

★
YOUR MOST
AWKWARD PHASE

_____
_____
_____
_____

★
THE MOST LIKELY TO
MAKE YOU LAUGH

_____
_____
_____
_____

★
THE MOMENT YOU
MISS THE MOST

_____
_____
_____
_____

★
THE SWEETEST TIME YOU
SHARED WITH SOMEONE ELSE

_____
_____
_____
_____

★
THE BEST
VACATION EVER

_____
_____
_____
_____

Collect your containers. Beautify your space. Organize your things. Take a deep breath.

You're done. How did it go? Capture your thoughts here:

_____
_____
_____

However you did, give
yourself a gold star.

ORGANIZING TOYS

RATE THIS MESS: ○ ○ ○ ○ ○

The last thing you want is for your living room to feel like a nursery. At the same time, when the kids are happy and occupied, the grown-ups tend to be happier, too. Cue: Compromise. If you don't have kids, use this challenge to focus on containing the "toys" that keep you occupied in your living room: remote controls, DVDs, puzzles, games, and movie-night paraphernalia.

THINGS YOU NEED TO GET RID OF

_____

_____

_____

_____

WHAT YOU WANT TO ACCOMPLISH WITH THIS PROJECT

_____

_____

_____

_____

THINGS THIS SPACE COULD USE

_____

_____

_____

_____

The Mice Will Play

1. Designate a specific area in the living room where the toys will live. This allows kids to develop a sense of ownership, and they will be less likely to move playtime to other areas of the home.

2. Contain the items in a way that simplifies the cleanup process. Bulky items (stuffed animals, trucks, train sets, etc.) can be stored in large floor baskets, so toys are concealed when playtime is over, but still accessible. Items like puzzles and games can be stacked neatly on a shelf—in rainbow order, of course!

3. Label each category and keep it general.

4. Use floor baskets for movie-night blankets— if a nearby closet isn't available, that is.

_____

_____

_____

_____

TRY IT! Did somebody say *movie*? (Ah, yes, we did!) List the toys and movies you loved when you were growing up.

_____   _____
_____   _____
_____   _____
_____   _____
_____   _____
_____   _____
_____   _____
_____   _____
_____   _____
_____   _____
_____   _____
_____   _____
_____   _____
_____   _____
_____   _____
_____   _____
_____   _____
_____   _____

Collect your containers. Beautify your space. Organize your things. Take a deep breath.

You're done. How did it go? Capture your thoughts here:

_____
_____
_____

However you did, give
yourself a gold star.

ARRANGING FURNITURE

RATE THIS MESS: ○ ○ ○ ○ ○

People think it's easy to arrange the furniture in the house, especially in the living room. Just plop it down and call it a day. But it takes more than spreading the furniture pieces randomly if you want to make a good impression. You want to balance your living room design in a way that feels welcoming and cozy, but also looks nice. You also want to allow for good flow throughout the room. We've got some thoughts on all this (no surprise). First, though, let's reflect.

THINGS YOU NEED TO GET RID OF

_____

_____

_____

WAYS TO BEAUTIFY THIS SPACE

_____

_____

_____

THINGS THIS SPACE COULD USE

_____

_____

_____

HOW YOU WANT TO FEEL WHEN SITTING HERE

_____

_____

_____

Change It Up

1. Find the wall plugs and avoid covering them with furniture. You want easy access to outlets for lamps and such.

2. Place the furniture evenly throughout the room. Weighing it too heavily to one side gives the impression of a sinking ship (remember the *Titanic*?).

3. Create a conversation area by, for instance, placing a sofa and two chairs around a coffee table. If your living room is large enough, try to move the conversation area away from the TV, or else pull attention from it by adding other things of interest, such as books on shelves and artwork on the wall.

4. Leave traffic lanes of at least twenty to twenty-four inches so people can walk around and through without bumping into things.

5. Mix fabric textures to keep things interesting. And if two different pieces share a design feature (metal details maybe?), they'll look like friends without being matchy-matchy twins, which is what you're going for.

TRY IT! This is one place where drawing a bird's-eye view of your living room really helps you avoid pushing furniture around unnecessarily and also allows you to know what you're missing. So grab your handy tape measure and be nerdy about this. Draw your room below (see page 7)—and don't forget to mark those outlets, too.

Collect your containers. Beautify your space. Organize your things. Take a deep breath.

You're done. How did it go? Capture your thoughts here:

However you did, give
yourself a gold star.

CHARGING STATION

RATE THIS MESS: ○ ○ ○ ○ ○

Are you one of the many people who panics when your phone gets below 50 percent battery life? And when the battery icon turns *RED*, do you start having heart palpitations? You're not alone. It's a common affliction, and there is a cure: charging stations. Let's create one in a corner or on an unused side table or anywhere else that works in your home.

THINGS YOU NEED TO GET RID OF

_____

_____

_____

_____

_____

THINGS YOU USE ONLY OCCASIONALLY

_____

_____

_____

_____

_____

THINGS THIS SPACE COULD USE

_____

_____

_____

_____

_____

Stay Plugged In

1. Use a multi-USB port to minimize the number of plugs going into the wall.

2. Route and wrap the cords to obscure them from view. Consider using cord covers that stick to the wall. This way, tablets and phones are able to power up without creating an eyesore in the surrounding space.

3. Line up the laptops, phones, and tablets with a letter divider so you can store them together while they're charging overnight.

_____

_____

_____

_____

_____

TRY IT! If you could hire a (very responsible) robot to do anything, what would it be? Drive your kid to early-morning swim practice? Do the laundry? Write your list here. No judgment.

Collect your containers. Beautify your space. Organize your things. Take a deep breath.

You're done. How did it go? Capture your thoughts here:

However you did, give
yourself a gold star.

CHAPTER 4

THE BATHROOM

Bathrooms are another one of our favorite rooms to organize. And I know you're thinking that we say *every* room is our favorite, but it's not true. Garages, basements, and attics—not so great. But a bathroom is SO FUN, and the possibilities are endless. Another nice thing about working on a bathroom is that the categories are pretty clear and generally consistent from home to home.

You will almost always be organizing your items into these groupings: face, hair, dental, and bath and body. If you're anything like us, you'll likely have these additional groupings: eyes, makeup, hair tools, cotton swabs and rounds, back-stock (back-up supplies), and travel items. If you can manage to get your basic categories grouped and organized, but you don't have the energy to sort them further, that is STILL a huge win. Fine-tune things later—you'd be amazed how easy it is to separate dry shampoo from hair spray while holding a glass of wine! Reflect on the following questions.

What's working for you in this space? What's not working?

_____

_____

_____

_____

How could this space be more functional? More beautiful?

_____

_____

_____

_____

How do you want to feel when you enter it?

_____

_____

_____

_____

What does this space need less of? What could it use more of?

_____

_____

_____

_____

THE DRAWERS

RATE THIS MESS: ○ ○ ○ ○ ○

If your bathroom lacks cabinet space, you can just as easily use a drawer. Almost all bottles can lie flat as opposed to standing upright—just make sure lids are on extra-tight. Our favorite bathroom drawer is the "daily" drawer, which contains the bathroom's greatest hits. These are your go-to items that you use twice a day without fail. Think toothbrush and toothpaste, contacts, face wipes—anything that's part of your regular routine. Don't have a bathroom drawer? Consider setting up a stand-alone drawer in a cabinet. The idea is to keep these items accessible so you can get ready and get out the door.

THINGS YOU NEED TO GET RID OF

_____

_____

_____

_____

_____

WAYS TO BEAUTIFY THIS SPACE

_____

_____

_____

_____

THINGS THIS SPACE COULD USE

_____

_____

_____

SOS (Save Our Skin)

A few ideas to keep your beauty must-haves looking, well, beautiful:

1. Anchor odd-shaped chargers and other tools in the corner of your drawer, opening up countertop space.

2. Group products by brand rather than category to keep sets together.

3. Distinguish Q-tips from cotton balls, using compartmented containers.

4. Use modular drawer organizers in varying sizes to separate your categories and contain any spills.

5. Place items used together next to one another in the drawer.

_____

_____

_____

TRY IT! Use the gridded paper below to plan out the space by drawing your drawer's dimensions (see page 7).

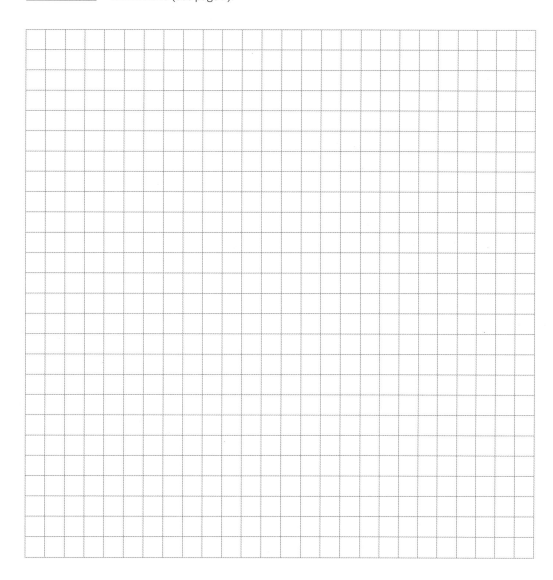

Collect your containers. Beautify your space. Organize your things. Take a deep breath.

You're done. How did it go? Capture your thoughts here:

_____

_____

_____

However you did, give
yourself a gold star.

UNDER THE SINK

RATE THIS MESS: ○ ○ ○ ○ ○

The space beneath the bathroom sink is just as important as the space under the kitchen sink and should not be ignored. In many instances, it's the best place to stand up large bottles of shampoo, hair products, lotion, and more, so put it to good use! And just because you bought it doesn't mean you have to keep it. It's a bummer, but sometimes products just aren't as effective as you expected. Those have got to go to make room for what you do use (and remember, you're much less likely to use something if you can't see it). Keep that in mind as you think through the type of under-the-sink drawers, shelves, and containers that will help you with this space.

THINGS YOU NEED TO GET RID OF

_____

_____

_____

_____

THINGS YOU NEED TO ACCESS
MORE EASILY

_____

_____

_____

THINGS THIS SPACE COULD USE

_____

_____

_____

_____

Go Deep

Extra-deep pull-out drawers take advantage of the sink depth.

Back-stock supplies of hair, face, and makeup products can be organized in separate containers.

Cups for storage in the makeup drawer keep small items from rolling around.

_____

_____

_____

_____

TRY IT! Use the gridded paper below to plan out your space by drawing the dimensions under your sink, considering the pipes (see page 7).

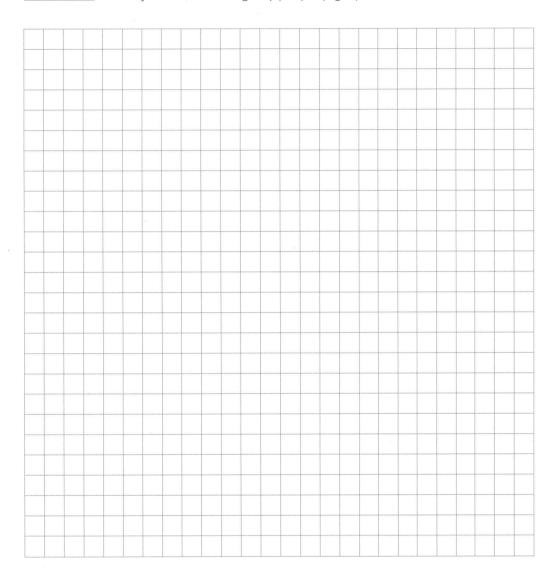

Collect your containers. Beautify your space. Organize your things. Take a deep breath.

You're done. How did it go? Capture your thoughts here:

_____

_____

_____

However you did, give
yourself a gold star.

THE SHELF

RATE THIS MESS: ○ ○ ○ ○ ○

Open shelving is usually reserved for things that are meant to be displayed, like neatly folded towels, pretty self-care supplies, and a candle or two. Extra bathroom products, on the other hand, are usually stashed out of sight, hidden behind cabinet doors and in drawers. But adding some elevated products and organizing everything into categories for display can make all the difference in this room.

THINGS YOU DON'T NEED TO KEEP HERE

_____
_____
_____
_____
_____

WAYS TO MAKE THIS SPACE PRETTIER

_____
_____
_____
_____

THINGS THIS SPACE COULD USE

_____
_____
_____
_____

All Clear

1. Store neatly contained, unopened back-stock supplies in clear bins on upper shelves.

2. Place bulky face- and hair-care products in concealed bins to mask the contents.

3. Put prettier items like nail polish and a manicure kit in take-along caddies.

_____
_____
_____
_____

_____
_____
_____
_____

List three products you can't live without.

_____

_____

_____

List three ways you can make your morning routine a bit more enjoyable.

_____

_____

_____

List three things you can do to ease your evening routine.

_____

_____

_____

Collect your containers. Beautify your space. Organize your things. Take a deep breath.

You're done. How did it go? Capture your thoughts here:

_____

_____

_____

_____

_____

However you did, give
yourself a gold star.

THE MEDICINE CABINET

RATE THIS MESS: ○ ○ ○ ○ ○

"**M**edicine" cabinets seem to hold a lot more than pills these days. Since these cabinets are often prime real estate in the bathroom, they tend to be used for products and supplies that you reach for on a daily basis (plus, they say you're not supposed to expose pills to heat and moisture, so . . .). In your nonmedicine medicine cabinet, for example, you could create a dedicated spot for everyday face products.

THINGS YOU NEED TO GET RID OF

_____

_____

_____

_____

_____

Divide and Conquer

1. Consider grouping items into categories like cleansers, moisturizers, and treatments.

2. Remove excess packaging to fit facial treatment packets in a space-saving bin.

3. Divide containers to help separate more specific subcategories.

WAYS TO SIMPLIFY THIS SPACE

_____

_____

_____

_____

_____   _____

_____

THINGS THIS CABINET COULD USE

_____   _____

_____   _____

_____   _____

_____   _____

Adding containers to a medicine cabinet is trickier than other spaces! Pay close attention to the depth of each shelf and the door hinges that might get in the way of your things. Then measure and draw your containers and items in the space below (see page 7). Remember: Medicine cabinet shelves are usually adjustable, so arrange them at will!

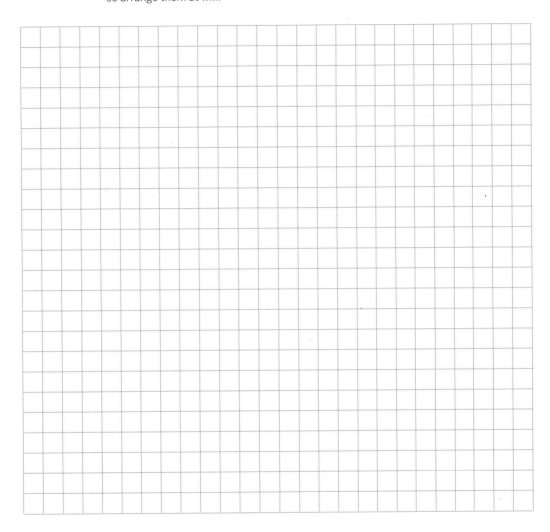

Collect your containers. Beautify your space. Organize your things. Take a deep breath.

You're done. How did it go? Capture your thoughts here:

_____

_____

_____

However you did, give
yourself a gold star.

THE COUNTERTOP

RATE THIS MESS: ○ ○ ○ ○ ○

Some people prefer to keep their makeup on the counter where they can see it, and some people *need* to make use of the countertop because they are short on storage space. If you fall into either of those buckets, stackable acrylic containers might change your life. Okay, maybe not your *life,* but certainly your bathroom.

THINGS YOU NEED TO GET RID OF

_____

_____

_____

_____

_____

_____

WAYS TO BEAUTIFY THIS SPACE

_____

_____

_____

_____

_____

THINGS THIS SPACE COULD USE

_____

_____

_____

On a Clear Day

1. Keep makeup in a single, clear, stackable storage or break up the components into a few different configurations—and remove individual sections while items are in use.

2. Line up products in each drawer so that the color of the label is visible whenever possible—this will make it is easy to find the product you need.

_____

_____

_____

_____

_____

_____

In your best handwriting, in big, beautiful script, write four motivational quotes here. Hey, while you're at it, tear out and post your favorite on your bathroom mirror.

Collect your containers. Beautify your space. Organize your things. Take a deep breath.

You're done. How did it go? Capture your thoughts here:

_____

_____

_____

However you did, give
yourself a gold star.

THE SUPPLY CABINET

RATE THIS MESS: ○ ○ ○ ○ ○

If you're lucky enough to have a supply cabinet or closet in your bathroom, you'll want to maximize it with storage bins that keep your items front and center. Once your spray bottles and first-aid supplies are neatly organized, you won't mind looking at them! We all need a spot in the home that holds the extra items we can't live without. Whether it's toilet paper and paper towels or diapers and cold medicine, you do *not* want to have to go to the store at eleven p.m. when you realize you're out of said item. Busy people need a lot of back-stock!

THINGS YOU NEED TO GET RID OF

_____

_____

_____

_____

WAYS TO MAXIMIZE STORAGE HERE

_____

_____

_____

_____

_____

THINGS THIS SPACE COULD USE

_____

_____

_____

_____

_____

Turn Around

It doesn't help to have all of your necessities stocked if you can't find them when you need them. That's when lazy Susans (aka turntables) can be helpful:

1. Arrange pharmacy and first-aid products on a turntable and in under-the-shelf organizers.

2. Use a turntable in a corner that's hard to reach and stock with lesser-used items, like Epsom salt.

3. Organize cleaning supplies on a turntable with toilet paper stacked neatly on either side to fill out the space.

_____

_____

_____

TRY IT! Is your household prepared in case of an emergency or a natural disaster? Not to sound alarming, but while you're organizing medical and pharmaceutical supplies, you might as well develop an action plan and discuss it with your family members. Do some research, then capture your ideas here.

OUR EMERGENCY CONTACTS:

NAME	NUMBER	EMAIL
NAME	NUMBER	EMAIL
NAME	NUMBER	EMAIL

Disasters most likely to strike in our area:

Second-best evacuation route outside of our neighborhood:

If we're separated or can't get home, here's where we should meet:

If we have to shelter in place at home, the best space for this is:

Best evacuation route outside of our neighborhood:

Other notes:

Collect your containers. Beautify your space. Organize your things. Take a deep breath.

You're done. How did it go? Capture your thoughts here:

However you did, give yourself a gold star.

THE LINEN CLOSET

RATE THIS MESS: ○ ○ ○ ○ ○

In theory, folded linens and towels would look perfect on an open shelf. Alas, there's the inconvenient truth that you don't live in a hotel or spa (YET . . . there's always hope), and it's never going to look as pristine when you try to replicate the stack of towels in your own home. But with the help of a few baskets, you'll get the look and save your sanity.

THINGS YOU NEED TO MOVE SOMEWHERE ELSE OR TOSS

_____

_____

_____

_____

_____

WAYS TO BEAUTIFY THIS SPACE

_____

_____

_____

_____

THINGS THIS SPACE COULD USE

_____

_____

_____

_____

Be Transparent

Some people might see a closet full of linens and panic. Not us. You just have to size the linens to the right containers. For example, you know what is similarly sized to a folded washcloth or linen napkin? A woman's shoe. A combination of stacking shoe dividers and clear shoeboxes can store all the varieties. Here are other ideas:

1. Consider investing in a bunch of wire baskets if you haven't already.

2. Divide your towels into categories, such as bath sheets, standard body towels, hand towels, and washcloths—and give each category its own neatly contained basket (with a lovely label, of course).

3. Use an additional basket to stack rows of toilet paper.

_____

_____

_____

TRY IT! Use the gridded paper below to plan out your linen closet by measuring your closet, then drawing its dimensions and sketching in your containers, towels, and other linens. Note which shelves can and should be adjusted to maximize your space (see page 7).

Collect your containers. Beautify your space. Organize your things. Take a deep breath.

You're done. How did it go? Capture your thoughts here:

_____

_____

_____

However you did, give yourself a gold star.

CHAPTER 5

THE HOME OFFICE/ STUDIO

Home offices are sometimes really enjoyable to work on, but sometimes . . . they are not. They're all just so different from home to home! Some offices we've worked on are studios for creative pursuits, some are for home businesses that operate out of a single room, and still others have documents dating back decades (ahem, those are not the fun ones). Whether you have a formal office or a nook in your home, organizing this space will help you organize your thoughts. Reflect on the following questions.

Most Important Things

_____

_____

_____

_____

_____

_____

_____

Least Important Things

_____

_____

_____

_____

_____

_____

_____

Ways to Make This Space More Pleasant

_____

_____

_____

_____

_____

_____

_____

ON THE DESK

RATE THIS MESS: ○ ○ ○ ○ ○

When organizing your desk, put the FUN in *functionality*. And by that we mean it's ROYGBIV to the rescue with your drawers, bins, and folders. That way your workday will be less, well, blue.

THINGS YOU NEED TO GET RID OF

_____

_____

_____

_____

_____

WAYS TO BEAUTIFY THIS SPACE

_____

_____

_____

_____

_____

THINGS THIS SPACE COULD USE

_____

_____

_____

_____

_____

Pack It Up

Some things you still need in your house, but don't want within arm's reach:

1. Store important documents safely in file boxes with hanging folders.

2. Pack up finished projects in labeled document boxes—and put them either on a shelf or, better yet, in the attic or basement, so they don't take up valuable real estate on your desk.

3. Use bins you can rotate in and out if your business changes seasonally.

4. Fill stackable clear drawers with electronics, cords, and printer paper—those can also go on a shelf to keep your desk clear.

5. Create a docking station for your daily electronics (phone, laptop, etc.), so you can unplug from your devices while your devices remain plugged in.

_____

_____

_____

We all have jobs—whether you leave every day for a nine-to-five or whether you're a stay-at-home parent. What part of your work brings you the most joy (and how can you do more of it)?

_____

_____

_____

_____

_____

_____

_____

_____

_____

_____

_____

_____

_____

_____

_____

_____

_____

Collect your containers. Beautify your space. Organize your things. Take a deep breath.

You're done. How did it go? Capture your thoughts here:

_____

_____

_____

However you did, give
yourself a gold star.

CREATIVE SUPPLIES

RATE THIS MESS: ○ ○ ○ ○ ○

Everyone should have pursuits that make them happy—we say the more creative the better. We love organizing spaces where you get to exercise your passions on a daily or weekly basis—especially if it's also how you earn a living. Right up our alley! ROYGBIV to the nth degree.

THINGS YOU NEED TO GET RID OF

_____

_____

_____

_____

WAYS TO BEAUTIFY THIS SPACE

_____

_____

_____

_____

THINGS THIS SPACE COULD USE

_____

_____

_____

_____

In Living Color

When shopping for products, think (literally) outside the box. Don't limit yourself by sticking to the "office section" when you might find even more useful supplies throughout the store. Walk down each aisle and get as many options as possible; you can always return what doesn't work. Remember: Clear eyes, full carts, can't lose.

1. Store paintbrushes in hairbrush holders, grouped by size and type.

2. Prop up paint bottles on three-tiered pantry shelves and line them up by type and hue for inspiration and convenience.

3. Use clear compartmented cases for all of your different bead varieties. The bigger the beads, the bigger the compartments.

4. Show off beautiful balls of yarn sorted by color in acrylic boxes.

_____

_____

_____

TRY IT! Think of a project or passion you want to pursue over the next year, then take 10 minutes to write about how you'll go about accomplishing it. You got this!

_____

_____

_____

_____

_____

_____

_____

_____

_____

_____

_____

_____

_____

_____

_____

_____

_____

_____

_____

_____

Collect your containers. Beautify your space. Organize your things. Take a deep breath.

You're done. How did it go? Capture your thoughts here:

_____

_____

_____

However you did, give yourself a gold star.

THE CABINET

RATE THIS MESS: ○ ○ ○ ○ ○

Scissors, pens, and stacks of paper have to live somewhere. So maximize those cabinets! You can turn any empty cabinet into a supply station.

THINGS YOU NEED TO GET RID OF

Cabinet Calls-to-Action

1. Store your ongoing projects in top-shelf baskets.

2. Stack white and colored paper in acrylic boxes.

3. Prop up scissors and brushes in oversize cups.

4. Compartmentalize caddies to keep school and art supplies tidy and separate.

WAYS TO BEAUTIFY THIS SPACE

THINGS THIS SPACE COULD USE

TRY IT! What accomplishments make you feel extremely proud?
List them here.

_____

_____

_____

_____

_____

_____

_____

_____

_____

_____

_____

_____

_____

Collect your containers. Beautify your space. Organize your things. Take a deep breath.

You're done. How did it go? Capture your thoughts here:

_____

_____

_____

_____

_____

However you did, give
yourself a gold star.

CHAPTER 6

THE ENTRYWAY

Entryways vary quite a bit from home to home. But what they all have in common is that every one of us enters our home through a door and needs a place where we can immediately put down our things. Even the tiniest apartment needs a hook on the wall or a spot for stashing keys and mail. As you answer these questions, take stock of all the items that enter and exit your house on a daily basis: backpacks, coats, hats, handbags, umbrellas, mail, keys, you name it. Then think about where it all naturally lands when you and your crew walk in. Do shoes pile up on the floor? Is there mail on the counter? It's best to find a system—and design solutions—that fit your space *and* your needs. Before we start, reflect on the following questions.

What's working for you in this space? What's not working?

_____

_____

_____

_____

_____

How could this space be more functional? More beautiful?

_____

_____

_____

_____

_____

How do you want to feel when you enter it?

_____

_____

_____

_____

_____

What does this space need less of? What could it use more of?

_____

_____

_____

_____

_____

THE TABLE

RATE THIS MESS: ○ ○ ○ ○ ○

We always say there are a few ways to keep your entryway looking picture-perfect at all times: Live alone, own nothing, or give your kids a separate entrance. Accept that this space will never stay perfect. But cleaning burns calories, so there's that!

THINGS YOU NEED TO GET RID OF

_____

_____

_____

_____

_____

WAYS TO BEAUTIFY THIS SPACE

_____

_____

_____

_____

_____

THINGS THIS SPACE COULD USE

_____   _____

_____   _____

_____   _____

_____   _____

Maxed Out

1. Place decorative objects on a tabletop to preempt any pileup of coats and handbags. Those belong on hooks or in a nearby closet.

2. Hide mail, keys, and sunglasses in the table's drawer, if there is one.

3. Tuck divided and labeled baskets under the table—one basket for each child to place his or her backpack and one basket with hanging files for papers.

4. Designate a decorative wastebasket for junk mail, so you can cast it aside as soon as you bring it through the door.

TRY IT! We try to be positive whenever possible, but we're human! Who doesn't have their pet peeves? List all of yours here.

_____

_____

_____

_____

_____

_____

_____

_____

_____

_____

_____

_____

_____

_____

_____

_____

_____

_____

_____

_____

Collect your containers. Beautify your space. Organize your things. Take a deep breath.

You're done. How did it go? Capture your thoughts here:

_____

_____

_____

_____

_____

However you did, give
yourself a gold star.

THE COAT CLOSET

RATE THIS MESS: ○ ○ ○ ○ ○

Just because it's a coat closet doesn't mean it has to hold only coats. As long as the items stay contained and labeled, they're free to crash the coat party. Extra entertaining supplies? You're invited. Sweaters? Sure, come along. You're in charge of the guest list, and it might help to start with some reflection.

THINGS YOU NEED TO GET RID OF

_____

_____

_____

_____

_____

Coat Closet Shopping List

Opaque bins to conceal loose entertaining supplies (in the front) and any supplies overstock (in the back)

Sturdy hangers for heavy coats

WAYS TO MAKE THIS CLOSET MORE FUNCTIONAL

_____   _____

_____   _____

_____   _____

_____   _____

THINGS THIS CLOSET COULD USE

_____   _____

_____   _____

_____   _____

_____   _____

On your way out? Grab your coat, but don't forget your grocery shopping list! Just a few things to pick up today . . . What are they?

_____   _____
_____   _____
_____   _____
_____   _____
_____   _____
_____   _____
_____   _____
_____   _____
_____   _____
_____   _____
_____   _____
_____   _____
_____   _____
_____   _____
_____   _____

Collect your containers. Beautify your space. Organize your things. Take a deep breath.

You're done. How did it go? Capture your thoughts here:

_____
_____
_____

However you did, give
yourself a gold star.

THE FLOOR

RATE THIS MESS: ○ ○ ○ ○ ○

Sometimes you try an organizing system, but it just doesn't work. This is not uncommon in the entryway. For example, let's say you set up a system with one coat hook for each family member. No matter how many times you ask, everyone keeps throwing their items on the bench. Face it: The hook system may just be too complex. Try tweaking it so it works with their natural impulses—and thus, instead of hooks, let them drop their things into lined baskets. They look nice on the floor and contain items in an entryway.

THINGS YOU NEED TO GET RID OF

_____
_____
_____
_____
_____

WAYS TO BEAUTIFY THIS SPACE

_____
_____
_____
_____
_____

THINGS THIS SPACE COULD USE

_____
_____
_____
_____

Ode to a Lined Storage Basket

We're big fans of lined storage bins for the entryway. Not only are they beautiful, but also:

They're durable and practical because the lining can be washed when needed.

Visually, they add a softer touch in a room that's usually so industrial by nature.

The fabric will protect knit scarves and gloves from getting snagged by baskets.

_____
_____
_____
_____

Home for the day? You deserve a break. Pour a glass of wine or tea, grab some colored pencils or crayons, and relax by coloring in the lines below.

Collect your containers. Beautify your space. Organize your things. Take a deep breath.

You're done. How did it go? Capture your thoughts here:

_____

_____

_____

However you did, give
yourself a gold star.

CHAPTER 7

THE PLAYROOM

While a playroom or kids' bedroom tends to have significantly more to organize than an entryway closet—and therefore sometimes is a bit overwhelming—just remember that you should tackle every organizational challenge the same way: Take everything out, group things together, edit the items down, and assemble the categories back into an organized, labeled, and sustainable system. That way things won't get too sticky (sometimes literally sticky—mmmm half-eaten lollipop). Reflect on the following questions.

What's working for you in this space? What's not working?

_____

_____

_____

_____

_____

How could this space be more functional? Less chaotic?

_____

_____

_____

_____

_____

How do you want to feel when you enter it?

_____

_____

_____

_____

_____

What does this space need less of? What could it use more of?

_____

_____

_____

_____

_____

THE CRAFT DRAWER

RATE THIS MESS: ○ ○ ○ ○ ○

W
e are highly organized, yet incredibly uncrafty people. Honestly, the thought of a bunch of tiny buttons or googly eyes carelessly strewn all over the playroom is rather unsettling. But if you're brave enough to allow those tiny bits and pieces into your homes, you're our hero. Let's get this space shipshape.

THINGS YOU NEED TO GET RID OF

_____

_____

_____

_____

_____

WAYS TO BEAUTIFY THIS SPACE

_____

_____

_____

_____

_____

THINGS THIS SPACE COULD USE

_____

_____

_____

_____

_____

_____

Keep 'Em Separated

Small containers are an ideal fit for shallow drawers. Beads, buttons, and other little bits are best organized in their own cups. (Tip: Dixie cups, cleaned yogurt containers, or teacups work well.) Then larger crafting supplies like stamps and pipe cleaners should line the sides. Some items will just be too big or numerous for a drawer. Think: colored pencils, crayons, Popsicle sticks—and, for those, we like clear canisters. Here are more ideas:

1. Separate craft supplies into two groups: "better in a canister" and "better in a drawer." There's no right or wrong answer, but if you have two different storage options, it's preferable to use both available.

2. Organize the bits and pieces into families between those two groups. For instance, tape, clips, and stickers all attach and adhere, so you might place them together.

3. Ban glitter from your home entirely. (Just kidding. That's optional, but we certainly wouldn't judge!)

TRY IT! How many cups will you need? Measure your craft cup drawer, calculate how many categories of drawer-friendly items you have, and go from there—sketching out your plans in the grid below (see page 7).

Collect your containers. Beautify your space. Organize your things. Take a deep breath.

You're done. How did it go? Capture your thoughts here:

_____

_____

_____

However you did, give
yourself a gold star.

THE GO-PLAY-OUTSIDE DRAWER

RATE THIS MESS: ○ ○ ○ ○ ○

We're always impressed when parents let their kids use messy art materials indoors, but we believe sidewalk chalk is called SIDEWALK chalk for a reason. To encourage a clean home, we put together this drawer near the back door to make it easy to grab supplies on the way OUTSIDE.

THINGS YOU NEED TO GET RID OF

_____

_____

_____

_____

_____

WAYS TO BEAUTIFY THIS SPACE

_____

_____

_____

_____

_____

THINGS THIS SPACE COULD USE

_____

_____

_____

Fresh Air

The number of round and rectangular containers you'll need depends on how much of each type of art supply you have—and what your kids gravitate to. Once you've gone through them (and edited out any items that are past their prime), you'll be able to assess the situation—and decide what you have already and what you need to buy.

1. Encourage your kids to grab items without assistance with cups of sidewalk chalk (organized in ROYGBIV order).

2. Hold your paint jars and brushes in rectangular cups.

3. Look for plastic containers—because they're easy to clean!

_____

_____

When's the last time you played outdoors? What did you do? Capture a memory of the day below.

_____

_____

_____

_____

_____

_____

_____

_____

_____

_____

_____

_____

_____

_____

_____

_____

Collect your containers. Beautify your space. Organize your things. Take a deep breath.

You're done. How did it go? Capture your thoughts here:

_____

_____

_____

_____

_____

However you did, give
yourself a gold star.

THE TOY CLOSET

RATE THIS MESS: ○ ○ ○ ○ ○

We have one core principle when organizing a space meant for kids: It has to be easy. We're talkin' easy for them to access by themselves, easy for them to put things away, and easy for adults to assist (after all, let's face it—duty will call). One of the ways we make it accessible is to use clear stacking storage with labels. The bins are lightweight and even suitable for little hands, and they provide all the visual cues needed to get the space cleaned up in a snap, like a Mary Poppins–style game.

THINGS YOU NEED TO GET RID OF

_____

_____

_____

_____

WAYS TO BEAUTIFY THIS SPACE

_____

_____

_____

_____

THINGS THIS SPACE COULD USE

_____

_____

_____

_____

All-Access Pass

1. Organize blocks, cars, trains, and LEGO sets into stackable shoeboxes in two sizes appropriate for the contents.

2. Separate toy cars by color for easy identification (aka avoiding the need to dump out all the bins to find the car they're looking for).

3. Fill cups with flash cards, since flash cards make homework just a little more fun.

4. Use bins on a closet shelf to hold the never-ending categories of doll-size outfits, tutus, and gymnastics uniforms.

_____

_____

_____

_____

TRY IT! A blue car box. A green car box. A red car box. A rainbow Magna-Tile box. A clear Magna-Tile box. You see where we're going with this, right? Then count out the number of boxes you have and how many you need. Time to sketch it out (see page 7)!

Collect your containers. Beautify your space. Organize your things. Take a deep breath.

You're done. How did it go? Capture your thoughts here:

_____

_____

_____

However you did, give
yourself a gold star.

THE STUDY STATION

RATE THIS MESS: ○ ○ ○ ○ ○

As kids get older, it becomes more necessary to have a designated spot for doing homework. One of our favorite ways to set up a working space is to install an Elfa wall unit with a desktop and open shelving. But any simple table will do. And, of course, we can't resist an opportunity for some rainbow accessorizing!

THINGS YOU NEED TO GET RID OF

_____

_____

_____

_____

_____

WAYS TO SIMPLIFY THIS SPACE

_____

_____

_____

_____

WAYS TO MAKE THIS SPACE MORE APPEALING TO KIDS

_____

_____

_____

_____

Bouncing Off the Walls

1. Display infrequently used coloring implements nicely on the top shelf.

2. Store tools, supplies, and colored pencils (organize them by ROYGBIV for a fun pop!) in pegboard containers.

3. Keep jars of pens, pencils, and highlighters extra-accessible since they're used so often.

4. Keep the computer monitor on risers for extra storage underneath.

5. Find a fun, decorative object like a terrarium and use it to store pretty, but rarely needed, supplies like washi tape.

THINGS THIS SPACE COULD USE

_____

_____

_____

_____

Whether you've decided to install a new study station or are repurposing a desk or table, draw the layout on the grid below so you can plan for the containers and organizers you might need (see page 7).

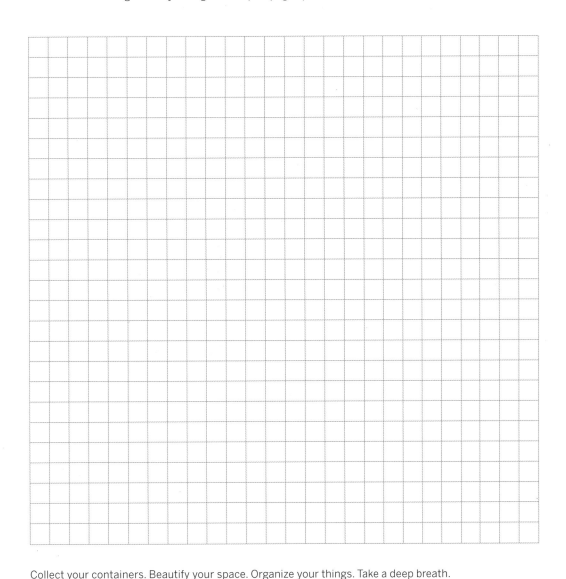

Collect your containers. Beautify your space. Organize your things. Take a deep breath.

You're done. How did it go? Capture your thoughts here:

_____

_____

_____

However you did, give
yourself a gold star.

UNDER THE STAIRS

RATE THIS MESS: ○ ○ ○ ○ ○

In the same way *The Wizard of Oz* gave everyone a healthy fear of tornadoes, Harry Potter didn't exactly provide positive press on closets under the stairs. So we want to firmly endorse using them to store all things *except* children. (Definitely don't do that.) But you *can* use them to store things your children *own*. (Definitely do that. And if you don't have stairs, use this time to organize the most awkward storage space in your home.)

THINGS YOU NEED TO GET RID OF

_____

_____

_____

_____

_____

Stairway to (Organizational) Heaven

WAYS TO BEAUTIFY THIS SPACE

1. Store surplus supplies (craft and otherwise) in extra-deep drawers (using the higher shelves for the things you need less often).

2. Place pens, pencils, markers, and stickers in open bins so they're handy.

3. Hold gift and party supplies in large, stacking drawers.

_____

_____

_____

_____

_____

THINGS THIS SPACE COULD USE

_____   _____

_____   _____

_____   _____

TRY IT! Take measurements and sketch some ways you could work with what you've got—maximizing the awkwardly shaped space (see page 7).

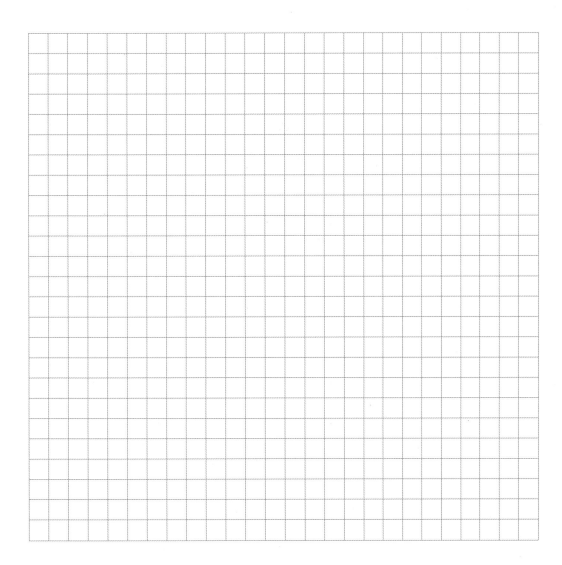

Collect your containers. Beautify your space. Organize your things. Take a deep breath.

You're done. How did it go? Capture your thoughts here:

_____

_____

_____

However you did, give
yourself a gold star.

CHAPTER 8

THE KIDS' BEDROOM

We think of ourselves as *very* fun moms. We say it's perfectly fine to own all the toys and games you want, but those items have to be properly contained and organized. The trouble in a kids' bedroom, though, is that a lot of the things have emotional significance for both you and your children. So it's a good time to remember The Home Edit basics (see opposite) and teach them to the next generation. Before we start, let's reflect.

What's working in this space? What's not working?

_____

_____

_____

_____

How could this space be more functional? More beautiful?

_____

_____

_____

_____

How do you want to feel when you enter it?

_____

_____

_____

_____

How do you want your kids to feel when they enter it?

_____

_____

_____

_____

What does this space need less of? What could it use more of?

_____

_____

_____

_____

BOOKS, GAMES & PUZZLES

RATE THIS MESS: ○ ○ ○ ○ ○

We're big fans of dividing a room, especially a kids' bedroom, into zones: homework station, makerspace, reading corner, arts and crafts, games and puzzles, and so on. Will that work in your home? Let's try it! Before we start, let's reflect.

WHAT'S WORKING FOR YOU IN THIS SPACE? WHAT'S NOT WORKING?

_____

_____

_____

_____

_____

HOW COULD THIS SPACE BE MORE FUNCTIONAL? MORE BEAUTIFUL?

_____

_____

_____

_____

_____

HOW DO YOU WANT TO FEEL WHEN YOU ENTER IT?

_____

_____

_____

_____

Made to Order

1. Line up books and stuffed animals near the bed so they're ready for downtime.

2. Put games, puzzles, science kits, and LEGO sets far away from the bed (if you can, depending on your layout), so they're ready to stimulate activity time.

3. Use magazine holders to organize workbooks, school papers, and homework folders.

4. Keep the floor clear by setting out playtime floor baskets where kids can throw their toys as they are done using them. This way, cleanup is more contained.

WHAT DOES THIS SPACE NEED LESS OF? WHAT COULD IT USE MORE OF?

_____

_____

_____

_____

_____

Maintaining The Home Edit systems throughout your home does *not* have to be a one-person job. We're all about the buddy system. (Can't you tell?) Whether you enlist your partner, kids, or roommate, we encourage you to delegate: You don't have to be in this alone (unless you want to be!). List some potential teammates here and the tasks they can handle.

_____   _____

_____   _____

_____   _____

_____   _____

_____   _____

_____   _____

_____   _____

_____   _____

_____   _____

_____   _____

_____   _____

_____   _____

_____   _____

_____   _____

_____   _____

Collect your containers. Beautify your space. Organize your things. Take a deep breath.

You're done. How did it go? Capture your thoughts here:

_____

_____

_____

However you did, give
yourself a gold star.

THE CLOSET

RATE THIS MESS: ○ ○ ○ ○ ○

Kids grow out of toys as quickly as they grow out of clothes. We recommend editing your kids' things twice a year (or more!) to clear out the clutter, especially before holidays or birthdays. Kids also tend to be natural hoarders—which means that culling their possessions can often turn into a temper tantrum. But it actually helps to get them involved so they understand that getting rid of those items will help them make room for what they do use and love. It's also a great way to start building healthy habits while teaching the importance of donating to those in need. Reflection time . . .

THINGS YOU NEED TO GET RID OF

_____

_____

_____

_____

WAYS TO BEAUTIFY THIS SPACE

_____

_____

_____

_____

THINGS THIS SPACE COULD USE

_____

_____

_____

_____

A Process Inspired by Cher Horowitz of Clueless

1. Pick out your children's favorite outfits.

2. Create a donate pile out of things your children have outgrown.

3. Snap photos of your kids' preferred "looks" and any shoes.

4. Print the pictures thumbnail-size (those trendy Mini Polaroids are perfect for this!).

5. Stick the shoe pics on the correct shoebox.

6. Stick the outfit pics on the closet door.

Think we are being excessive?
You'll thank us later!

_____

_____

This room can be Sentimentality City. If you're finding something hard to throw away, but don't want to keep it, try writing about it—how it came into your life, why it was meaningful, your favorite details. That way it won't be gone for good—you'll have memorialized it right here.

_____

_____

_____

_____

_____

_____

_____

_____

_____

_____

_____

_____

_____

_____

_____

_____

_____

_____

Collect your containers. Beautify your space. Organize your things. Take a deep breath.

You're done. How did it go? Capture your thoughts here:

_____

_____

_____

_____

_____

However you did, give
yourself a gold star.

CHAPTER 9

THE LAUNDRY ROOM

Doing laundry isn't at the top of our list of favorite activities, but organizing a laundry room is our idea of a good time. Whether you live alone or have a large family, this room is constantly used, and it greatly benefits from functionality. Having a laundry room that's not a headache can make washing and folding a little less unpleasant. Before we start, reflect on the following questions.

What's working for you in this space? What's not working?

_____

_____

_____

_____

_____

How could this space be more functional? More beautiful?

_____

_____

_____

_____

_____

How do you want to feel when you enter it?

_____

_____

_____

_____

_____

What does this space need less of? What could it use more of?

_____

_____

_____

_____

_____

THE SHELF

RATE THIS MESS: ○ ○ ○ ○ ○

Every laundry room needs at least one shelf to hold all the essentials. Put it to good use and you'll find there's nothing you can't handle. Even if you don't have a dedicated laundry room, try allocating a single shelf to holding detergent, softener, and stain removers.

THINGS YOU NEED TO GET RID OF

_____

_____

_____

_____

WAYS TO BEAUTIFY THIS SPACE

_____

_____

_____

_____

_____

THINGS THIS SPACE COULD USE

_____   _____

_____   _____

_____   _____

_____   _____

_____   _____

Space Invaders

1. Use lidded glass jars for detergent. They cost next to nothing AND you can perfectly see when it's time to restock.

2. Stock up on open bins—they're your best bet for everyday cleaning and laundry items like stain remover spray.

3. Reserve concealed lidded bins for extra household supplies (that somehow always find their way to the laundry room), like sunscreen and WD-40.

What's on your to-do list right now? Get it out of your brain by writing it here and make a plan for tackling at least one of the items today.

Collect your containers. Beautify your space. Organize your things. Take a deep breath.

You're done. How did it go? Capture your thoughts here:

However you did, give
yourself a gold star.

THE CABINET

RATE THIS MESS: ○ ○ ○ ○ ○

Doing laundry is kind of . . . terrible. But imagine a world where you enjoy a little moment of Zen every time you open your laundry room cabinet to grab the detergent. We're not saying that feeling will last beyond the spin cycle, but every little bit helps.

THINGS YOU NEED TO GET RID OF

_____

_____

_____

_____

_____

For a Crisp Cleaning Cabinet

Small, white containers for grab-and-go sponges

Plastic white bins with handles that can be wiped down in a pinch

Large white containers for detergents

Shelf heights adjusted to maximize space

Oversize black removable sticker labels to contrast with white containers

WAYS TO BEAUTIFY THIS SPACE

_____

_____

_____

_____

WAYS TO MAKE THIS SPACE
MORE FUNCTIONAL

_____   _____

_____   _____

_____   _____

_____   _____

_____   _____

When it comes to labels, don't be shy! Make your letters big and bold wherever you can. One may be specifically for "Ironing," for example; make those letters superclear so you never spend any time searching. Using the space below, practice writing out five new labels for your laundry categories, then make them happen IRL.

Collect your containers. Beautify your space. Organize your things. Take a deep breath.

You're done. How did it go? Capture your thoughts here:

However you did, give
yourself a gold star.

THE DOOR

RATE THIS MESS: ○ ○ ○ ○ ○

We REALLY like using a door for extra storage. It always feels like a magic trick because you get to store more things without them taking up additional space. You will *also* probably notice in this book that we get really excited about things that might be questionable on the excitement scale—but such is the life of a professional organizer. Space and storage just really get our blood pumping. For this challenge, consider investing in a hanging rack or other organizer for any door in your home.

THINGS YOU NEED TO GET RID OF

_____

_____

_____

_____

_____

Opportunity Is Knocking

1. Keep overstocked items at the top, since they don't need to be constantly accessible.

2. Organize smaller items like rags in shallow door baskets.

3. Place sprays and cleaning solutions in deep door baskets or pockets, where they fit perfectly.

WAYS TO MAXIMIZE THE STORAGE

_____

_____

_____

_____

_____   _____

_____   _____

THINGS THE DOOR COULD USE

_____   _____

_____   _____

_____   _____

_____   _____

What are three things you're really good at?

1. _____
_____
_____
_____

2. _____
_____
_____
_____

3. _____
_____
_____
_____

Collect your containers. Beautify your space. Organize your things. Take a deep breath.

You're done. How did it go? Capture your thoughts here:

_____
_____
_____
_____

However you did, give
yourself a gold star.

HAMPERS

RATE THIS MESS: ○ ○ ○ ○ ○

Not everyone has a laundry room that is large enough to host a high school dance. No matter what size this space is, you're going to want to keep it organized. Otherwise, it can easily turn into the room equivalent of a junk drawer! And for that, hampers are really helpful. Today's challenge is simple but has big rewards. We want you to rethink your laundry hampers: their size, location, and how you collect dirty clothes for the washing machine.

YOUR CURRENT HAMPER SYSTEM

_____

_____

_____

_____

_____

WHAT'S WORKING AND WHAT ISN'T

_____

_____

_____

_____

_____

IMPROVEMENTS YOU WANT TO MAKE

Simplify the Gathering and Sorting

Before you even get to the washing machine, it's important to create a laundry system that sets up all your family members for success. Here are a few ideas:

1. Label hampers by family member.

2. Use hampers with wheels.

3. Sort clothes by color.

4. Set aside delicates.

_____   _____

_____   _____

_____   _____

_____   _____

TRY IT! Doing laundry isn't so bad when you can tune out. What are your ten favorite songs of all time? Write out a playlist that includes these songs to enjoy the next time you do laundry.

1. _____

2. _____

3. _____

4. _____

5. _____

6. _____

7. _____

8. _____

9. _____

10. _____

Collect your containers. Beautify your space. Organize your things. Take a deep breath.

You're done. How did it go? Capture your thoughts here:

_____

_____

However you did, give
yourself a gold star.

CHAPTER 10

THE GUEST AREA

Setting up a guest area is fun because you can include things you wouldn't use yourself on a daily basis. Go ahead and splurge so they feel like royalty. Before we start, reflect on the following questions.

What's working for you in this space? What's not working?

_____
_____
_____
_____

How could this space be more inviting?

_____
_____
_____
_____

How do you want your guests to feel when they enter it?

_____
_____
_____
_____

What does this space need less of? What could it use more of?

_____
_____
_____
_____

THE BEDROOM

RATE THIS MESS: ○ ○ ○ ○ ○

One way to make your guests feel like they're at a hotel? A self-serve morning station. That way, if they're awake first, they don't have to wait for you to get a bite to eat and their hot bevvy fix (and psst, you get to sleep a little longer). You could do this on a dresser or small table, so it doesn't need to take up a lot of space—and it's a real crowd-pleaser.

THINGS YOU NEED TO GET RID OF

_____

_____

_____

_____

_____

_____

_____

_____

THINGS THIS AREA COULD USE

_____

_____

_____

_____

_____

_____

_____

Buzz Buzz Buzz

A few ideas for making guests feel at home:

1. Find an empty surface or shelf for setting up a self-serve morning station. Consider a small coffee maker and electric kettle for hot water.

2. Organize one or two mugs nearby—on a shelf is one possibility—for quick access.

3. Add coffee pods or grounds and tea bags, plus some pouches of instant oatmeal and breakfast bars, in clear jars with labels for each type, like "Decaf" and "Caffeinated."

4. Include a water pitcher for refilling the coffee maker and a tray for transporting drinks to the bed.

_____

_____

_____

_____

Think back to your best guest experience at someone else's home. What made it special? How can you incorporate some of those ideas into your own guest space?

_____

_____

_____

_____

_____

_____

_____

_____

_____

_____

_____

_____

_____

_____

_____

_____

Collect your containers. Beautify your space. Organize your things. Take a deep breath.

You're done. How did it go? Capture your thoughts here:

_____

_____

_____

_____

_____

However you did, give
yourself a gold star.

THE BATHROOM

RATE THIS MESS: ○ ○ ○ ○ ○

When you're on vacation, what supplies are you really excited to see in the bathroom? Fancy toothpaste? Moisturizers with amazing scents? The floss and razor you forgot to pack? Once everyone's turned in, your guests will be so relieved not to have to knock on your door to ask for the things they left behind. When converting a standard bathroom to a guest bathroom, consider . . .

THINGS YOU NEED TO GET RID OF

_____

_____

_____

_____

_____

Drawer and More

1. Line up bath and body products with in-drawer dividers to hold everything in place.

2. Arrange travel-sized toothpastes by ROYGBIV.

3. Compartmentalize other dental, shave, cotton, and face supplies.

WAYS TO BEAUTIFY THIS SPACE

_____

_____

_____

_____

_____

THINGS THIS ROOM COULD USE

_____

_____

_____

_____

List your top five travel destinations and what you'd like to do there:

1. _____

   _____

2. _____

   _____

3. _____

   _____

4. _____

   _____

5. _____

   _____

Collect your containers. Beautify your space. Organize your things. Take a deep breath.

You're done. How did it go? Capture your thoughts here:

_____

_____

_____

However you did, give
yourself a gold star.

CHAPTER 11

THE MUDROOM

Not everyone has a standard mudroom (which generally includes built-in stalls and hooks and cubbies), but if you do have an everyday entrance to your home, you know that space can feel like the equivalent of Grand Central Terminal with a steady stream of traffic coming through the door. Because everyone uses this space heavily, it's a good idea to designate a spot for each member of the family. This will hold each person accountable for his or her own space. Let's reflect . . .

What's working for you in this space? What's not working?

_____
_____
_____
_____
_____

How could this space be more functional? More beautiful?

_____
_____
_____
_____
_____

How do you want to feel when you enter?

_____
_____
_____
_____
_____

What does this space need less of? What could it use more of?

_____
_____
_____
_____
_____

THE SHELVES

RATE THIS MESS: ○ ○ ○ ○ ○

The mudroom is one of those spaces where a solid system can shave precious minutes off your morning routine when you're trying to get out the door to school, work, or wherever. Here's a good place to start:

THINGS YOU NEED TO GET RID OF

_____

_____

_____

_____

_____

WAYS TO BEAUTIFY THIS SPACE

_____

_____

_____

_____

_____

THINGS THIS SPACE COULD USE

_____

_____

_____

_____

_____

_____

High Shelves for Items Needed Less Often

Laundry supplies

Household items

Tools

Extra towels

Bulky items

Low Shelves for Easy-to-Grab Items

Winter accessories

Outdoor supplies (like the dog leash)

Essentials for after-school activities (in designated baskets)

When chores are feeling overwhelming, sometimes it helps to make (and follow!) an official schedule. Jot down some ideas below for when your family will do what during the week. Bonus points for involving everyone in this planning!

M _____

_____

T _____

_____

W _____

_____

Th _____

_____

F _____

_____

S _____

_____

Su _____

_____

Collect your containers. Beautify your space. Organize your things. Take a deep breath.

You're done. How did it go? Capture your thoughts here:

_____

_____

However you did, give
yourself a gold star.

THE MULTIPURPOSE CLOSET

RATE THIS MESS: ○ ○ ○ ○ ○

We like to take *full* advantage of every square inch of storage. If you have a front hall closet or a storage closet, consider all the categories you might be able to store in it. In this case, we love fitting coats, shoes, rain gear, pharmacy supplies, and utility items by creating zones for each category so you know exactly where to find everything.

THINGS YOU NEED TO GET RID OF

_____

_____

_____

_____

_____

THINGS YOU NEED EASIER ACCESS TO

_____

_____

_____

_____

_____

THINGS THIS SPACE COULD USE

_____

_____

_____

_____

Full Spectrum

1. Line the top shelf with extra utility and household items, like lightbulbs.

2. Stock pharmacy, wellness, and first-aid products in clear bins for full visibility.

3. Store two or three pairs of shoes for each member of the family in clear shoeboxes.

4. Organize summer and winter items in floor baskets labeled by season.

_____

_____

_____

_____

TRY IT! This space can benefit from some planning and extra shelves and hanging rods. Measure your closet and use the grid below to plot out where you'll store everything in this area (see page 7).

Collect your containers. Beautify your space. Organize your things. Take a deep breath.

You're done. How did it go? Capture your thoughts here:

_____

_____

_____

However you did, give
yourself a gold star.

BEACH THINGS

RATE THIS MESS: ○ ○ ○ ○ ○

When summer rolls around, you might find it helpful to rearrange your mudroom—or should we call it a *sand*room?—to accommodate all of those fun outdoor activities for the park, beach, or pool. Instead of hats and mittens, find a system for storing all of that sunscreen and those pairs of goggles.

TYPE OF SYSTEM YOU THINK WOULD
WORK BEST HERE

_____

_____

_____

_____

_____

WAYS TO BEAUTIFY THIS SPACE

_____

_____

_____

_____

_____

THINGS THIS SPACE COULD USE

_____

_____

_____

_____

Surf and Turf

1. Store extra straw hats and rolled beach towels (yes, rolled!) on shelves to grab quickly on the way to the beach or the pool.

2. Keep outdoor sprays and sunscreens, extra hats, sunglasses, and beach supplies in bins.

3. Set out lightweight baskets for shoes on the bottom shelf.

_____

_____

_____

_____

_____

What beach reads are on your list right now?

_____

_____

_____

_____

_____

_____

_____

_____

_____

_____

_____

_____

_____

_____

_____

_____

Collect your containers. Beautify your space. Organize your things. Take a deep breath.

You're done. How did it go? Capture your thoughts here:

_____

_____

_____

_____

_____

However you did, give
yourself a gold star.

SPORTS THINGS

RATE THIS MESS: ○ ○ ○ ○ ○

Some people say, "winter, spring, summer, fall." Others say, "hockey, basketball, baseball, soccer." Athleticism doesn't run in either of our families, but we've still picked up a few tips and tricks here and there. Hopefully we can help you apply them to *your* space—wherever you decide to store all of those sports items. Let's get started.

THINGS YOU NEED TO GET RID OF

_____

_____

_____

_____

_____

WAYS TO MAKE THIS SPACE MORE FUNCTIONAL

_____

_____

_____

_____

_____

THINGS THIS SPACE COULD USE

_____

_____

_____

_____

Zone Defense

If you opt for an indoor setup (instead of, say, the garage), consider a cubby system. All the bulky items are in concealed baskets, and the shelves contain everything from golf balls to shin guards. And if each team requires different jerseys or footwear, just remember to label them as such!

1. Sort all sports equipment and divide it into zones.

2. Think of storage solutions in terms of the shapes of the sports accessories. For example, utility racks normally reserved for mops and brooms work perfectly for baseball bats.

3. Store additional gear and outdoor items in adjacent drawers or floor bins.

_____

_____

_____

_____

TRY IT! Regardless of where you decide to store your sports items, use your tape measure to see how much space you have to work with and sketch out some ideas in this grid (see page 7).

Collect your containers. Beautify your space. Organize your things. Take a deep breath.

You're done. How did it go? Capture your thoughts here:

However you did, give
yourself a gold star.

PET THINGS

RATE THIS MESS: ○ ○ ○ ○ ○

For many animal lovers, one just isn't enough. But that also means twice the amount of supplies. In order to keep your home from turning into a boarding kennel, it's important to add storage solutions before things get out of hand. We like stackable bins and turntables (aka lazy Susans) on a top shelf for toys. But wait. There's more . . .

THINGS YOU NEED TO GET RID OF

_____

_____

_____

_____

_____

Dog (or Cat) Days

1. Decide on a room or a space for your pet supplies.

2. Group the categories—grooming, treats, toys, first aid, outdoor, etc.—and separate them into bins.

3. Designate the location of each bin based on usage (keep treats up high!).

4. Try storing smaller items in deep drawers, using dividers to give each group a home.

5. Use cabinets for litter supplies—they work well for items you don't need to access as often.

WAYS TO REWORK THIS SPACE

_____

_____

_____

_____

_____

THINGS THIS SPACE COULD USE

_____   _____

_____   _____

_____   _____

_____   _____

TRY IT! Measure your pet area really well to see how all the turntables and bins will lay out best—or what you have to work with in that deep drawer. Sketch your plans below (see page 7).

Collect your containers. Beautify your space. Organize your things. Take a deep breath.

You're done. How did it go? Capture your thoughts here:

_____

_____

_____

However you did, give
yourself a gold star.

CHAPTER 12

ON-THE-GO SYSTEMS

―――――

This chapter hits a little too close to home. Although what do we know about being close to home? If we spend more than two weeks in town, it's a miracle. The only thing that helps us get through our day-to-day work life is a series of finely tuned systems. This chapter is all about travel: We're going to organize your car, your bag for your daily commute, your luggage, and your phone. Before we start, reflect on the following questions.

What's working—and not working—for you when you're on the go?

_____

_____

_____

_____

_____

How could you simplify these areas of your life?

_____

_____

_____

_____

_____

How do you want them to make you feel?

_____

_____

_____

_____

_____

What do you need more of? Less of?

_____

_____

_____

_____

_____

THE CAR

RATE THIS MESS: ○ ○ ○ ○ ○

While organizing your own trunk, consider what you might need to have on hand for your kids or pets, and what activities require you to have some supplies ready for use. Thinking through your lifestyle and its participants will help you sort out what you might want to designate specifically for your car.

THINGS YOU NEED TO GET RID OF

_____

_____

_____

_____

WAYS TO MAKE YOUR CAR STORAGE MORE FUNCTIONAL

_____

_____

_____

_____

THINGS YOUR CAR COULD USE

_____

_____

_____

_____

Possible Car Contenders

Organizing the trunk of your car is as simple as getting a collapsible organizing case and packing it with the items you need most often. Here's our list of essentials and extras:

Essentials

PAPER TOWELS

HAND TOWEL

EXTRA JACKET

PAIR OF ATHLETIC SHOES

UMBRELLA

Extras

BLANKET

CHANGE OF CLOTHES (FOR YOU AND/OR YOUR KIDS)

DOG LEASH

EXTRA PHONE CHARGER

HAIRBRUSH

HAT

SNACKS (NOTHING THAT MELTS)

SUNGLASSES

SUNSCREEN

YOGA MAT

Road trip! Think back to the vacations you've taken by car and answer the following questions.

What's the longest car trip you've taken? Was it a family tradition growing up? Were you visiting family?

_____

_____

_____

_____

_____

_____

_____

What is your dream road trip—the national parks? Coast-to-coast?

_____

_____

_____

_____

_____

_____

_____

Collect your containers. Beautify your space. Organize your things. Take a deep breath.

You're done. How did it go? Capture your thoughts here:

_____

_____

_____

However you did, give
yourself a gold star.

THE CARRYALL

RATE THIS MESS: ○ ○ ○ ○ ○

Whether you're prepping your handbag or an airplane carry-on, nothing helps with organization like interior pouches.

THINGS YOU NEED TO GET RID OF

_____
_____
_____
_____
_____
_____

Put These Ideas in the Bag

ONE CASE FOR YOUR LAPTOP, TABLET, EARBUDS, AND CHARGERS

ONE CASE FOR COSMETICS

ONE CASE FOR SUNGLASSES

ONE CASE FOR PHARMACY NECESSITIES

ONE CASE FOR SNACKS

WAYS TO FIND ITEMS MORE EASILY

_____
_____
_____
_____
_____
_____

THINGS YOUR BAG COULD USE

_____ _____
_____ _____
_____ _____
_____ _____

TRY IT! What are a few of your favorite on-the-go snacks? (We love low-carb tortillas. Don't knock 'em till you've tried 'em!)

Collect your containers. Beautify your space. Organize your things. Take a deep breath.

You're done. How did it go? Capture your thoughts here:

However you did, give
yourself a gold star.

THE LUGGAGE

RATE THIS MESS: ○ ○ ○ ○ ○

We often say we have only one true skill: organizing. But lately, it seems appropriate to add "expert packers" to our résumés. Here are our secrets to keeping it all contained on the go.

TRAVEL ITEMS YOU NEED TO GET RID OF

_____

_____

_____

_____

_____

TRAVEL ITEMS YOU NEED

_____

_____

_____

_____

_____

WAYS TO MAKE YOUR LUGGAGE MORE FUNCTIONAL

_____

_____

_____

_____

_____

Opportunity Is Knocking

1. Consider packing cubes, which are a travel game changer and make packing and unpacking your suitcase so much easier. The trick is finding a set that fits what you regularly travel with.

2. Use mesh tops for your clothing. They are designed to ventilate, but they also allow you to clearly see what you have. As long as you file-fold your items so that they stand upright rather than stacking them, you can easily grab what you want without rummaging through a pile.

3. Employ opaque cases for more discreet items, like undergarments. No need for TSA to literally air your dirty laundry.

4. Select specialty cases for things like extra shoes or jewelry.

5. Use toiletry bags with a lot of zippered pouches—ideally made of water-resistant material in case something leaks!—to secure their contents.

This task involves making a packing list that covers the trips you take the most. Not all items will apply to all trips, but no matter where you're going, you can run through this go-to list and check off the applicable items. You might even annotate your packing lists to indicate what you did and didn't wear and use on the trip, so that your future lists will be more relevant to your needs. Start by jotting down some thoughts below on items you want to include.

_____   _____
_____   _____
_____   _____
_____   _____
_____   _____
_____   _____
_____   _____
_____   _____
_____   _____
_____   _____
_____   _____
_____   _____
_____   _____
_____   _____
_____   _____
_____   _____

Collect your containers. Beautify your space. Organize your things. Take a deep breath.

You're done. How did it go? Capture your thoughts here:

_____
_____
_____

However you did, give
yourself a gold star.

THE PHONE

RATE THIS MESS: ○ ○ ○ ○ ○

If you already have an organized phone, it's likely grouped by app type: social, news, travel, etc. And that's totally fine, if that works for you! But typically, a good bit of scrolling and scanning is still required to find the app you need, since you don't have easy visual recognition. This is why we think ROYGBIV is the only way to go when organizing the apps on your phone. App icons are not arbitrarily picked; they are intentionally designed to be recognized and remembered among a sea of other apps. The human brain is able to easily recognize things visually in the same way muscle memory develops: by repetition and use. If you use your apps, you already know what they look like. If you don't use them, then you should delete them.

APPS YOU NEED TO GET RID OF

_____

_____

_____

_____

_____

_____

This Is How We Do It

1. Edit. We *all* have apps we don't use (us included). Get rid of any that are outdated or unused, since they only clutter your screen.

2. Group. Place your apps into folders organized by color.

3. Sort. Within each folder, place your most commonly used apps at the very top so you can spot them immediately. (App arrangement within the color folder is a critical part of why this system works.)

4. Label. Instead of labeling your folders "Red" or "Blue," pick an emoji that color coordinates with the apps in the folder.

WAYS TO MAKE YOUR PHONE EASIER TO NAVIGATE

_____

_____

_____

_____

_____

_____   _____

_____   _____

_____   _____

Use the space below to design an emoji: your face, your home, *our* faces (be kind), whatever you want.

Organize your apps and take a deep breath.

You're done. How did it go? Capture your thoughts here:

_____

_____

_____

However you did, give
yourself a gold star.

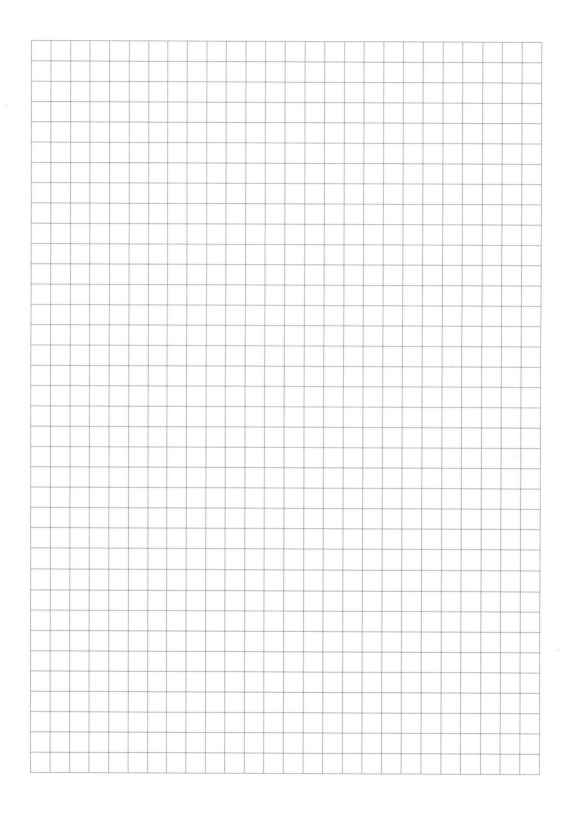

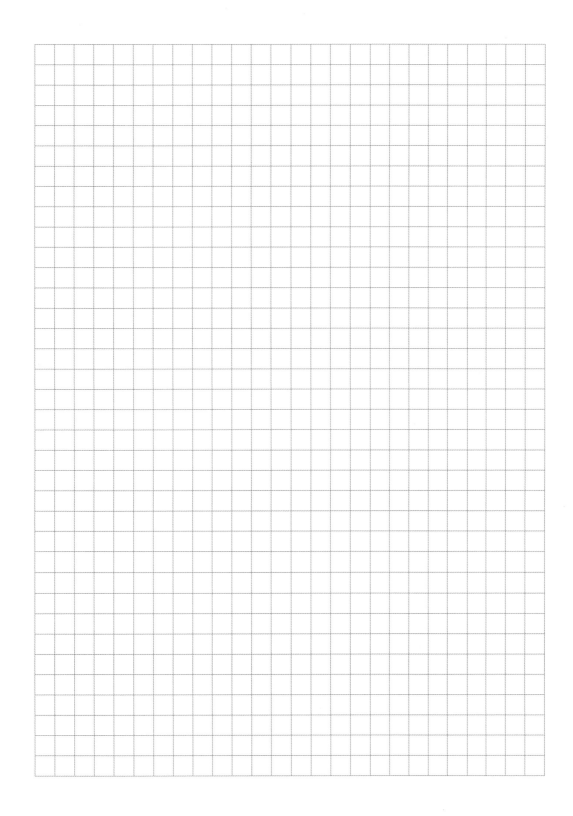

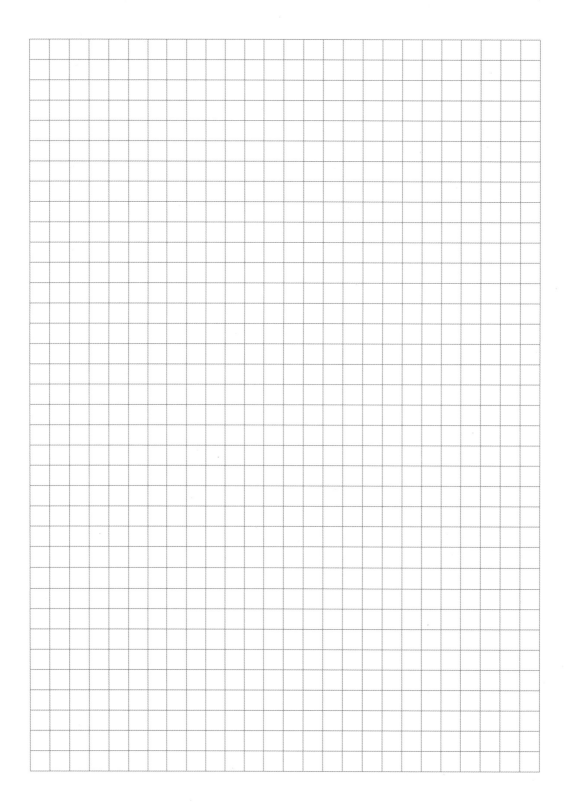

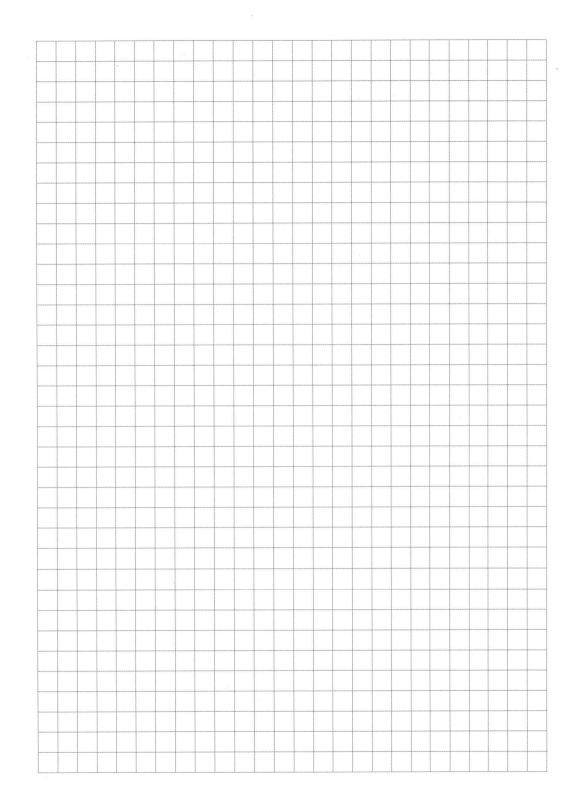

Copyright © 2019, 2020, 2021 by The Home Edit Print, LLC

All rights reserved.
Published in the United States by Clarkson Potter/
Publishers, an imprint of Random House, a division of
Penguin Random House LLC, New York.
clarksonpotter.com

CLARKSON POTTER is a trademark and POTTER with
colophon is a registered trademark of Penguin Random
House LLC.

Selected materials originally appeared in the following:
The Home Edit by Clarkson Potter/Publishers, an imprint
of Random House, a division of Penguin Random House
LLC, New York, in 2019, and *The Home Edit Life* by Clarkson
Potter/Publishers, an imprint of Random House, a division
of Penguin Random House LLC, New York, in 2020.

ISBN 978-0-593-13982-0

Printed in China

Design by Mia Johnson and Jennifer K. Beal Davis
Illustrations by Mia Johnson

10 9 8 7 6 5 4 3

First Edition